DON TROIANI'S CIVIL WAR
Infantry

Art by Don Troiani

Text by Earl J. Coates, Michael J. McAfee, and Don Troiani

STACKPOLE
BOOKS

Published in paperback in 2006 by
STACKPOLE BOOKS
5067 Ritter Road
Mechanicsburg, PA 17055
www.stackpolebooks.com

Printed in China

10 9 8 7 6 5 4 3 2 1

FIRST EDITION

For free information about the artwork and limited edition prints of Don Troiani, contact:

Historical Art Prints
P.O. Box 660
Southbury, CT 06488
203-262-6560
www.historicalartprints.com

For information on licensing images in this book, visit www.historicalimagebank.com

Library of Congress Cataloging-in-Publication Data

Troiani, Don.
    [Don Troiani's regiments and uniforms of the Civil War. Selections]
    Don Troiani's Civil War infantry / art by Don Troiani ; text by Earl J. Coates, Michael J.
McAfee, and Don Troiani.— 1st ed.
            p. cm.
    Reprints a portion of the author's Don Troiani's regiments and uniforms of the Civil War.
Mechanicsburg, PA : Stackpole Books, c2002.
    ISBN-13: 978-0-8117-3318-2
    ISBN-10: 0-8117-3318-1
    1. United States. Army. Infantry—History—Civil War, 1861–1865—Pictorial works. 2. United
States. Army. Infantry—Uniforms—History—19th century—Pictorial works. 3. Confederate States
of America. Army—Infantry—Pictorial works. 4. Confederate States of America. Army—Infantry—
Uniforms—Pictorial works. 5. Soldiers—United States—History—19th century—Pictorial works. 6.
Soldiers—Confederate States of America—History—Pictorial works. 7. United States—History—
Civil War, 1861–1865—Regimental histories. 8. United States—History—Civil War, 1861–1865—
Pictorial works. I. Title: Civil War infantry. II. Coates, Earl J. III. McAfee, Michael J. IV. Title.
E492.4.T76 2006
973.7'8—dc22
                                                                    2005027477

INTRODUCTION

THIS BOOK IS TAKEN FROM THE LARGER VOLUME *Don Troiani's Regiments and Uniforms of the Civil War* to provide a less expensive reference source for those interested in specific areas of Civil War uniforms. The subject of Civil War infantry could not be comprehensively covered in one hundred small volumes such as this, but this publication will provide a good overview.

The foot soldiers of the Civil War were the men who ultimately won or lost the battles. To most, the North wore blue, and the South gray, but it was not nearly so simple in reality. Governments, states, and private contractors manufactured an almost endless array of styles of clothing, using an equally varied assortment of textiles and colors. Often, there were significant differences between a garment made by one depot and the same item made by another. Some clothing was based on regional availability and yet others on imported goods. Here, we have shown some of the most typical—and also some of the most interesting and unusual—dress of the Civil War infantryman.

My longtime friends, Earl J. Coates and Michael J. McAfee, represent the pinnacle of their fields in research, and working with them has always been an enjoyable and enriching experience. Contributing authors Tom Arliskis and David M. Sullivan, also leaders in their areas of study, presented fresh information and ideas. Working with primary source materials, period photography, and original artifacts gave us the opportunity to explore the dress of many units from a multi-dimensional perspective. Equally important was the wise counsel offered by some of the great Civil War collectors and students of material culture: James C. Frasca, John Henry Kurtz, Paul Loane, Dean Nelson, Michael O'Donnell, and John Ockerbloom, among many others. Their decades of practical hands-on experience provided knowledge that cannot be "book learned."

Posing fully dressed models for all the studies in the book also opened the vista of seeing what some of this stuff really looked like on the soldier. Reading about it is one thing; seeing it is quite another.

As the main topic is uniforms, we have not explored firearms or edged weapons as they are exhaustively covered by many other books. We have touched on accoutrements but not in anything approaching complete coverage, selecting mostly items that augmented illustrated uniforms.

In researching the figure studies, the authors consulted every available source. Despite our more than a hundred years of combined study, we recognize that there's a good chance that another interesting nugget of new or conflicting data, perhaps from an unpublished account or collection, could surface after this book's publication. But that is the way of historical research and, indeed, one of the facets that makes it both frustrating and fascinating. To those who are disappointed that a favorite regiment has been left out, please forgive me, I'll try to get to it in the future!

Don Troiani
Southbury, Connecticut

ACKNOWLEDGMENTS

I DEDICATE THIS BOOK TO MY FATHER, DOMINICK H. Troiani (1916–2005), 258th Field Artillery, HQ Company, 95th Infantry Division, who served his country in France and Germany in 1944–45. His war stories got me interested in all this as a child. I also dedicate it to all the gallant servicemen and women who continue to defend our country on a daily basis.

I owe a debt of gratitude to my distinguished friends Earl J. Coates and Michael J. McAfee, two of the greatest gurus on the subject of Civil War uniforms, who graciously tolerated all my ceaseless questions and, as always, shared the fruits of a lifetime research with me. They are genuinely "national treasures." Particular thanks to contributing authors Tom Arliskis, who provided important primary information on Western units, and David Sullivan renowned authority on Civil War marines.

Special credit to renowned Civil War author-photographer Michael O'Donnell for taking many of the fine color photos of artifacts for this book, and to Tracy Studios of Southbury, Connecticut.

The following individuals and institutions also contributed to the creation of this book: Gil Barrett, Bruce Bazelon, Carl Borick, Robert Braun, William Brayton, Major William Brown, William L. Brown III, Christopher Bryant, Rene Chartrand, Charles Childs, Dr. Michael Cunningham, Ray Darida, Dr. David Evans, William Erquitt, Robin Ferit, James C. Frasca, Joseph Fulginiti, Fred Gaede, Holly Hageman, Charles Harris, Randy Hackenburg, Gary Hendershott, Bruce Hermann, Steven Hill, Robert Hodge, Mark Jaeger, Les Jensen, James L. Kochan, Robert K. Krick, Michael Kramer, John Henry Kurtz, John P. Langellier, William Lazenby, Claude Levet, Paul C. Loane, Edward McGee, Bob McDonald, Steven McKinney, Howard M. Madaus, Michael P. Musick, Dean Nelson, Donna O'Brien, John Ockerbloom, Stephen Osmun, Col. J. Craig Nannos, Dean Nelson, Larry Page, Andrew Pells, Ron Palm, Nicholas Picerno, the late Brian Pohanka, Cricket Pohanka, Kenneth Powers, Shannon Pritchard, Pat Ricci, Steven Rogers, Nancy Dearing Rossbacher, A. H. Seibel Jr., Mark Sherman, Sam Small, Wes Small, James R. H. Spears, Steve Sylvia, Brendan Synonmon, William Synonmon, David Sullivan, Donald Tharpe, Mike Thorson, Warren Tice, Ken Turner, William A. Turner, Cole Unson, James Vance, Michael Vice, Gary Wilkensen, Don Williams, and Michael J. Winey.

The Booth Museum of Western Art, Cartersville, Georgia; Confederate Memorial Hall, New Orleans; Charleston Museum, Charleston, South Carolina; Connecticut Historical Society; Connecticut State Library; New York State Collection; Pamplin Historical Park and the National Museum of the Civil War Soldier; Middlesex County Historical Society; The Company of Military Historians; the Nelsonian Institute; *North South Trader* magazine; The Horse Soldier; The Union Drummer Boy; and the West Point Museum, United States Military Academy.

The Infantry

WITH ONLY A FEW EXCEPTIONS, THE OUTCOME of every major battle in the American Civil War was decided by the soldiers who fought on foot with handheld weapons—the infantry. Their skill and determination, combined with the leadership ability of those commanding them, made the difference on such fields as Manassas, Shiloh, Antietam, and Gettysburg. But skill, determination, and even devotion to a cause are not always enough to assure final victory. A nation must be able to equip, feed, clothe, and maintain the means of supplying her armies for the duration of the conflict. Upon this rests the chance for ultimate victory. History has shown that when a country loses this capability—by enemy intervention, a lack of resources, or a combination of the two—little, short of a major military blunder by her enemy, will prevent disaster.

When war began in April 1861, the two contending factions were ill equipped to cope with the demands of a struggle that was destined to last more than the few months envisioned at the time. Sending soldiers to fight one or two major, decisive battles was one thing; sustaining them in the field for a prolonged period was another. To do so required factories and facilities capable of turning out arms, munitions, equipment, and clothing. Raw materials were also necessary to supply these factories, and food was needed to feed the men, who made up the fighting force, and their animals. Although arms and most leather accoutrements would last for extended periods if cared for, the average uniform of a Civil War soldier in the field lasted only a few months. On a long campaign, such as Gettysburg, the infantry soldier often wore out one or two pairs of shoes from lengthy marches on rough roads. Marching also wore out trousers, the continual friction wearing holes in the legs as well as on the hips, where equipment, particularly the cartridge box, rubbed. In

1861, the professional soldiers who made up the high command of both the Union and Confederate armies, unlike many of the state and national politicians, knew well the needs they would face.

Whereas many of the best combat officers of the prewar U.S. Army resigned their commissions to serve the Confederacy, it is an often overlooked fact that, with only few exceptions, those responsible for supplying that army stayed with the Union. Prior to the outbreak of the war, the uniforms of the U.S. Army had been manufactured and supplied by a single facility, Schuylkill Arsenal, in Philadelphia. This facility was staffed and maintained by the army's Quartermaster Department, which was also responsible for getting the uniforms and other supplies to an army that, though small in numbers, was spread across the entire country. In addition, the cloth that went to make the uniforms for the army came from a single factory—the Utica Steam Woolen Company in Utica, New York.

The uniform style worn by the Federal army in 1861 had been adopted in 1858 and was to a large extent patterned after that worn by the French. By army regulation, the infantry soldier was issued a total of eight coats, seven caps, thirteen pairs of trousers, fifteen shirts, eleven pairs of drawers, twenty pairs of stockings, and twenty pairs of shoes over a five-year enlistment. Based on this regulation and years of experience, the quartermasters were able to accurately estimate the annual needs of the army, even to how many of each size garment were likely to be called for. Large numbers of uniforms were not made in advance and stockpiled, so the Schuylkill Arsenal facility could and did respond quickly to special requests. In the late 1850s, a winter expedition against the Indians in the Northwest prompted a call for overcoats with hoods instead of the regulation cape, as well as cavalry

2

Detail of coat sleeve of Col. John B. G. Kennedy of the 5th Louisiana Battalion (later Kennedy's 21st Louisiana Regiment). The Austrian-inspired gold tape sleeve knots denote the rank of colonel, and the dark blue velvet cuff trim indicates the branch of service, in this case infantry. Kennedy, a veteran of the Mexican War, commanded the unit until the summer of 1863, when most of the men were transferred into the 1st Louisiana and he was assigned to the C.S.A. Quartermaster Department. TROIANI COLLECTION.

boots with lower heels for infantry wear. These were readily supplied with no questions asked.

With the coming of war, tens of thousands of volunteers took the field in uniforms supplied by their native states. These quickly wore out, and the majority of those who had been mustered into the service of the Federal government now looked to that authority to supply their needs. Drawing on the years of experience of its senior officers, the U.S. Army Quartermaster Department moved quickly to meet the challenge. Meeting the demand necessitated contracting with existing clothing houses. The ready-to-wear clothing industry was in its infancy, but the westward expansion of the country had created a demand for clothing that was mass-produced and not made by local tailors or at home. New York, Cincinnati, and St. Louis had commercial clothing manufacturing facilities, as did Philadelphia. It was in these areas that the army first established branch clothing depots. Of these, both Cincinnati and St. Louis began actual manufacturing operations, while New York was run as a contracting depot drawing on the existing local industry, which actually extended north to Boston. As the war progressed, other, smaller branch depots were opened, most notably in Steubenville, Ohio, and Quincy, Illinois.

The situation was far more desperate in the Confederacy. Having fewer textile mills and no facility such as Schuylkill Arsenal to use as a base, the South was forced to start from scratch. Initially the Confederate government elected to begin a commutation system that called for the volunteers to supply their own uniforms to be paid for by the government. The small Confederate Regular army alone was uniformed by the government. The system resulted in uniforms of widely varying quality and styles, although by the end of 1861, the color gray was generally accepted as standard.

It did not take long, however, before reality set in. The uniforms received by many Southern soldiers did not hold up under conditions in the field. It is likely that here the enduring myth of the ragged Confederate soldier was born. It was evident that some government control was essential. If the initial determination of the Confederacy to exist as a separate nation can be seen anywhere, it is in the rapid expansion of its economy to a wartime footing. The establishment of an arms-making industry is well documented, but the equally impressive development of a system of depots to manufacture uniforms and accoutrements is often overlooked. An initial depot in Richmond, which was opened in September 1861, was eventually expanded to include depots in Nashville and Memphis, Tennessee; Athens, Atlanta, and Columbus, Georgia; Charleston, South Carolina; Marion, Montgomery, and Tuscaloosa, Alabama; Enterprise, Mississippi; Shreveport, Louisiana; Little Rock, Arkansas; and San Antonio and Houston, Texas. Not all of these operated for the entire war; some, in fact, did so only for a few months. Nevertheless, the list represents a monumental effort to ensure that the Confederate soldier was well clothed and well equipped.

Once the supply of uniforms and clothing was stabilized in both the Union and the Confederacy, the problem for soldiers in the field in general switched from one of standardiza-

Although trousers were issued by the government, suspenders were not. Therefore, it was up to the individual soldier to find a means of keeping up his pants. The solution was civilian suspenders of every conceivable color combination and ornamentation available. This striped pair was used by a Connecticut soldier during 1862–63. TROIANI COLLECTION.

tion and quality to one of supply. Without careful planning, rapidly moving armies can easily outdistance their supply lines. Between early 1862 and early 1865, there were times when the soldiers of both armies were in uniforms that were well worn. Often uniform supply was dependent on the efficiency and knowledge of regimental or brigade quartermasters, many of whom brought little or no experience to the job. Because of this, ample evidence brings into question the stereotypes of the always ragged Rebel and the ever well-clothed and well-equipped Yankee. Photographs of well-uniformed Confederate dead or captured of the Army of Northern Virginia taken in 1863 and early 1865 clearly open to question the idea of undersupplied soldiers. And an inspection report of New York's famed Excelsior Brigade, dated July 27, 1863, states that "the men are sadly in need of clothing which should be supplied prior to a march, both as a sanitary measure and economy of strength."[1]

Clothing depots in both the North and South supplied uniforms to all branches, but sheer volume dictated that the vast majority of the items made or contracted for went to the infantry. Geographic location of the depots dictated to a great extent which of the field commands would draw on which depot.

From late 1862 until the collapse of the Confederate supply system in the final months of the war, there were numerous similarities in the manufacture and supply of uniforms and equipment to the Union and the Confederate infantry. Both were at times troubled with substandard material, both suffered at times from inefficient supply officers, but conversely, during this period, both generally provided clothes and adequate equipment to their soldiers. Though there were some similarities in uniform style, there were also differences that made the infantrymen of the North and the South as distinct and dissimilar as the causes for which they were fighting.

It is difficult to describe a "typical" infantry soldier of either the Union or Confederate army. Except for a small number of Regulars in the Federal army, both forces were composed of volunteers, men who valued independence and individuality. They at times either ignored or found creative ways to circumvent standardization orders that seemed to them superficial. The appearance and equipment of the men in both armies evolved during the war to the point that the typical soldier of 1861 would have been an oddity to the veterans who marched and fought on the fields of Virginia or Georgia in 1864.

This Federal forage cap bears the blue cloth crescent badge of the 3rd Division, XI Army Corps. Adopted March 21, 1863, the badge was used until the XI Corps was consolidated with the XII to form the XX Army Corps in April 1864. JOHN OCKERBLOOM COLLECTION.

HEADGEAR
Union
The Federal army issued two types of headgear to its infantry enlisted men: the pattern 1858 army hat and the pattern 1858 forage, or fatigue, cap. During peacetime, all soldiers received both—the hat for dress occasions and the cap for general use. But in wartime, economy and practical necessity made the continued issue of both a rare occurrence. In general, the Federal soldier received only the cap, though the hat was favored by some, most notably the Iron Brigade. In some commands, soldiers were allowed to purchase and wear hats similar to the army hat; these were shaped to suit the individual. By the latter part of the war, this practice was far more prevalent in the Western armies than in the East. In both Eastern and Western armies, however, many commanders preferred the fatigue cap. In the Army of the Potomac, numerous orders issued in 1864 called for all nonissue headgear to be confiscated and in some cases burned. An order issued to the 53rd Pennsylvania Infantry, near Petersburg, Virginia, September 4, 1864, for example, said, "Every enlisted man in the Regiment must be provided with a cap.... In the future any man appearing on duty with hats on will be sent to their companies and others detailed instead and both the officers in command of the Companies and the men themselves held accountable. The officers placed in arrest and the men punished accordingly."[2]

Confederate
For Confederate regiments in both theaters of the war, there was a much greater variety and acceptance of various patterns of headgear than in the Union armies. Although in some regiments hats seem dominate, the issuance of caps was widespread. For example, requisitions for the 19th Alabama Infantry throughout 1863 and early 1864 show a decided preference for hats, whereas those for the 17th Mississippi Infantry for the same period record only caps being received.[3] One Confederate clothing facility in Charleston, South Carolina, was devoted entirely to the manufacture of caps. These were cut out by government employees at the depot and sent to 1,000 to 1,500 local "persons of a needy class" for assembly.[4]

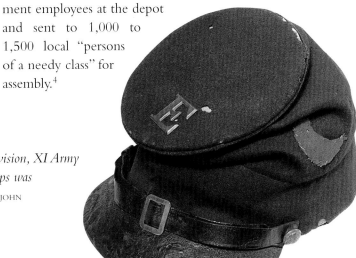

Late-war Richmond Depot–produced jacket worn by Pvt. John K. Coleman of the 6th South Carolina Infantry in 1865. Earlier patterns produced by this depot were ornamented with tape trim or featured belt and shoulder straps. GARY HENDERSHOTT.

Confederate "forked-tongue" brass waist belt buckle found near Sequatchie Valley, Tennessee. One of the most widely used buckles in all theaters of the war, this specimen exhibits an interesting field-made replacement tongue. CHARLES HARRIS COLLECTION.

COATS, BLOUSES, AND JACKETS

Union

In the Regular army, enlisted infantrymen received both a frock coat for dress purposes and a fatigue blouse to be worn on other occasions. As large numbers of volunteers filled the ranks, supplying both to each man sometimes stretched the capability of the quartermasters. As production problems stabilized, however, many volunteers did in fact receive both. In the early part of the war during the summer campaign, overburdened infantrymen often threw away extra clothing to lighten their loads, so as spring approached in 1863, 1864, and 1865, the soldiers emerging from winter quarters were ordered to put excess clothing in storage. If both the frock coat and fatigue blouse had been issued, which would be worn was usually decided within the regiment, and at times within the company. Although the majority wore the much lighter and more comfortable blouse, many chose to march and go into battle in the frock coat. In addition, many New York units were issued and wore waist-length jackets from the state for a good part of the war. In some cases, troops brigaded with New York units appear to have received such jackets. The 5th Michigan Infantry, which was in the same brigade of the III Corps with the 40th New York, received a small number of these jackets in early 1863.[5]

Confederate

The Confederate army began the war with uniform coats that were anything but uniform. Differences in style and color often existed within the same regiment. By mid-1863, despite some continued acquisition of frock coats, expediency had forced the Confederate army to settle on a nearly universal issue of a gray waist-length jacket for the infantry. It was here, however, that the uniformity ended. There was little overall coordination among the various depots in either cut or trim of the jacket, and the type of material varied greatly in quality and composition. All wool was desired for durability, but it was common practice for Confederate uniforms to be made of a material referred to as jean, which was woven with a wool weft and a cotton warp. Dye lots varied greatly with availability, and some uniforms that started as gray quickly faded to tan or brown. As a result, the actual color of Confederate uniforms ranged from shades of brown to dark gray.

To supplement depot manufacture, the Confederate government was able to import both manufactured garments and cloth from abroad, but this material also varied in quality. In December 1863, Capt. James L. Tait of the British Army visited the South and offered to see to it that the Confederate army was supplied with uniforms of the very best quality. His offer was to supply, among other uniform items, 50,000 suits consisting of jacket and trousers "to be ready for shipment in 3 months from 1st January 1864."[6] The jackets and other items received were manufactured by the firm of Peter Tait of Limerick, Ireland, and were, as Captain Tait promised, of the very best quality cadet gray cloth. Few, if any, of these fine jackets reached the troops in areas other than Virginia and North Carolina.

TROUSERS

Union

In the period prior to the Civil War, the army-issue trouser was dark blue, the same color as the coat. On January 2, 1862, the commander of the Schuylkill Arsenal depot received word from the office of the quartermaster general that the color of trousers for regimental officers and enlisted men would be sky blue, and that the trouser stripe for noncommissioned infantry officers would now be dark blue.[7] The trousers for all branches were to be made of a durable, heavy woolen material known as kersey. Despite their durability, the trousers of the infantrymen required replacement several times during a season of heavy campaigning. No summer-weight trousers were issued, but natural properties of the kersey allowed for a certain level of comfort, even in hot weather.

The color change from dark to light blue prompted numerous complaints by the Regular army. As late as January 1863, the officer in charge of the Frankfort Arsenal was still trying to obtain dark blue for the enlisted men of his command. The change, however, would last until the army abandoned the blue uniform in the latter part of the nineteenth century.

Confederate

The trousers of the Confederate infantry were similar in cut and style to those of the Union army. Early Confederate regulations established the color for enlisted men's trousers as sky blue, and numerous existing examples give evidence that this color was used to some extent throughout the entire war. Far more common were the same shades of gray and brown seen in jackets issued to the Southern army. Confederate trousers were often made of the same wool-cotton jean cloth used for the jackets, though some were made entirely of cotton.[8] If the heavy wool of the Federal trousers wore out quickly, it is not surprising that the Confederate soldier was often seen marching through towns in ragged trousers. The extended campaign to Pennsylvania and back in 1863 took a heavy toll on uniforms, particularly trousers. Once the Army of Northern Virginia was back on Confederate

soil, regular replacements began to arrive. A typical example is Company E of the 53rd Virginia Infantry, one of Armistead's command, which, after the campaign, between July 31 and the end of the year, received 135 pairs of replacement trousers.[9]

FOOTWEAR

Union

It is unlikely that any other single item of army issue caused as much concern and problem as the shoes worn by the infantry. The standard army shoe or bootee was made of oak-tanned leather. It had four sets of eyelets and extended over the ankle. Although some infantrymen managed to acquire and wear boots, shoes were by far the standard for dismounted men. On campaign, they were often the first items to wear out. Next to running out of ammunition, the inability to replace a soldier's shoes was the greatest potential threat to his ability to function, and poor-quality footwear was often received from contractors and issued to soldiers. In one case, the assistant inspector general of the XI Army Corps reported on July 27, 1863, that "the last issue of shoes to this Corps received . . . at Frederick, Md. [are] of an inferior quality not lasting more than two or three weeks."[10]

Confederate

The supply of shoes to the Confederate army was a continuing and serious problem. Confederate footwear ranged from unavailable to barely adequate to some of the very best obtainable. A private of Company F, 53rd Virginia Infantry, served through the entire Antietam campaign in bare feet, later dying from a resulting infection.[11] At times, soldiers with skill as shoemakers were detailed from regiments in the field to make shoes from hides that had been secured by brigade or division quartermasters. Some shoes issued had cloth uppers attached to leather soles.

By 1863, some fortunate Southern soldiers received English shoes that had been run through the Federal naval blockade. These were described by a Union quartermaster as "the best I have seen for Army use." These shoes, which fastened with a strap and buckle instead of string, were well sewn and reinforced with nails, with a thin band of iron nailed to the bottom of the heel to prevent wear.[12]

Issued by the hundreds of thousands, there are few surviving examples of the Union army soldier's standard brogans today. This pair was worn by Sgt. Gilbert Bentley of the 37th Massachusetts Volunteer Infantry during the Appomattox, Virginia, campaign of 1865. TROIANI COLLECTION.

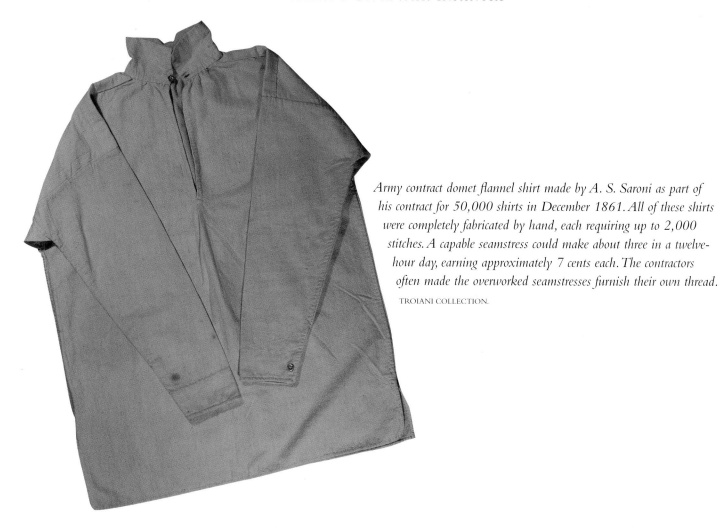

Army contract domet flannel shirt made by A. S. Saroni as part of his contract for 50,000 shirts in December 1861. All of these shirts were completely fabricated by hand, each requiring up to 2,000 stitches. A capable seamstress could make about three in a twelve-hour day, earning approximately 7 cents each. The contractors often made the overworked seamstresses furnish their own thread.
TROIANI COLLECTION.

SHIRTS
Union

The shirt issued by the U.S. government before and during the war was made of white domet flannel, a cotton and wool material. This pullover shirt was issued in a single size, with a single button at the neck and one at each cuff. The design made for ease of construction and certainly made requisition a simple matter of ordering enough to fill the need without regard to fit. During 1863, gray material was ordered as a secondary standard. From that date on, both were distributed on about an equal basis. Union soldiers are seen in numerous photographs in various styles and patterns of civilian shirts that were privately obtained; however, the use of civilian clothing by soldiers was discouraged and at times strictly forbidden.

Confederate

Confederate shirts can best be described as nondescript, as many, if not most, were privately obtained. Regimental records do, however, show regular issue of shirts of wool as well as cotton from the Quartermaster Department. An issue to the 4th Georgia Infantry in February 1863 shows both, with wool shirts charged to the soldier at $2 and cotton at $1.[13] Among the best received by the Confederate soldier were the blue-striped British Army issue, which came through the blockade.[14] The shirts, which likely accompanied

the large purchase of jackets and other items from Peter Tait in 1864, were described in the original letter sent to the secretary of war as "strong gray flannel."[15]

DESIGNATING INSIGNIA
Union

The Union infantry soldier, with few exceptions, was required to wear some manner of insignia, usually on his cap or hat, to allow quick and ready identification of the command to which he belonged. This insignia took the form of brass numbers to show his regiment, along with a brass letter to indicate the company within a regiment. In addition, some regiments also issued and required the soldier to wear a brass device shaped like a hunting horn, which was the U.S. Army designating device for infantry. Regiments that wore the model 1858 army hat usually used all three; those wearing the cap often dispensed with the horn. Photographs indicate that the wearing of designating insignia in the Western armies was not as strictly enforced as in the East.

Corps Badges

One of the most enduring insignia to emerge from the Civil War was the distinctive badges intended to designate each army corps. These corps badges were first used by the Army of the Potomac in the spring of 1863. Indifferently received by the soldiers when first issued, they soon became a symbol

Unusual soldier field-made VI Army Corps badge of painted oilcloth, worn by Cpl. Arthur P. Benner of Company I, 6th Maine Volunteer Infantry. TROIANI COLLECTION.

This folding Federal officer's slouch hat, worn by Maj. Ethan A. Jenks of the 7th Rhode Island Volunteers, has a maker's label in the lining reading, "Warburton's/Army Hat/Patented Dec. 16—1862—Made Expressly for/CL Lockwood, Washington, D.C." JOHN OCKERBLOOM COLLECTION.

of pride that carried over into the era of veterans' reunions and monument erection in the postwar years.

The original order for corps badges came from headquarters, Army of the Potomac, on March 21, 1863:[16]

> For the purposes of ready recognition of Corps and Divisions in this Army & to prevent injustice by reports of straggling & misconduct through mistake as to the organizations, the Chief Quartermaster will furnish without delay the following badges to be worn by the officers & enlisted men of all the Regiments of the various Corps mentioned.
>
> They will be securely fastened upon the centre of the top of the cap. Inspecting Officers will at all inspections see that these badges are worn as designated.

1st Corps . . . A Sphere (Red for 1st Division, White for 2nd Div., Blue for 3rd Div.)

2nd	"	a Trefoil	"	"	"
3rd	"	a Lozenge	"	"	"
5th	"	a Maltese Cross	"	"	"
6th	"	a Cross	"	"	"

(Light Div. Green)

| 11th | " | a Crescent | " | " | " |
| 12th | " | a Star | " | " | " |

The sizes and colors will be according to pattern.

By command of Maj. Gen. Hooker

Over the course of the war, corps badges were adopted by the entire Union army, although some corps did not adopt or use them until the final months of the conflict.

An order issued by the 1st Brigade, 2nd Division, XII Corps, on April 25, 1863, was repeated many times by other commands in the Army of the Potomac: "Hats will not be worn by the men when caps can be procured. Sutlers must be required to keep on hand letters and figures that each man may have the letter of his Company and number of his Regiment on the top of his cap, the White Star must also be worn on top of the cap."[17]

Confederate

Confederate soldiers received no designating insignia from the army. Some photographs show various devices affixed to the headgear of Southern soldiers. These were either privately obtained or purchased by a few Confederate regiments.

CORPORAL, 16TH NEW YORK INFANTRY, JUNE 1862

The 16th New York Infantry was raised in the far northern counties of the state in the weeks following the firing on Fort Sumter. Like many early regiments, it took the field under a regimental designation that reflected local pride, as well as the belief that this would be a short war—the 1st Northern New York Infantry. On May 15, 1861, the volunteers were mustered into U.S. service for two years as the 16th New York Infantry.

One month later, the regiment received its first issue of uniforms. Like other New York regiments, the 16th was outfitted by the state with the dark blue jacket adopted by New York in 1861, along with sky blue trousers and a fatigue cap of dark blue. Unlike other regiments that fought at First Bull Run or other early battles, there was no mistake that these were Union soldiers. But less than a year later, the 16th suffered heavy casualties, inflicted in part because of a change to this uniform.

As with numerous early war regiments, both Union and Confederate, many of the officers were local men of wealth and influence. On June 13, 1862, a letter written from the camp of the 16th New York near New Bridge, Virginia, read as follows: "I send you a photograph of Major Joel J. Seaver, of the 16th, he is a splendid fellow and all like him socially. He has just presented to each member of the regiment a nice straw hat, with a ribbon round it, on which is printed the number of the regiment in gilt letters and figures. The officers hats are bound with black, the others have no binding. He has given to the regiment rubber and woolen blankets, leggings, hats, flags and new instruments for the regimental band." Although the straw hats doubtless were a good deal more comfortable than the army-issue cap, they also proved to have a major disadvantage. The author of the regimental history of the 20th New York recalled of the 16th: "Before the Seven Days Battle the entire regiment [had received] white straw hats with wide brims. They wore these in the battle and were so conspicuous that the Rebels deliberately trained

TIM OSTERHELD

their cannons on them." Despite this, the 16th continued to wear the hats during the retreat to Harrison's Landing.

The 16th had initially been armed with M1840 smoothbore muskets. These, however, were replaced in July 1861 by Enfield rifle muskets supplied by the state of New York.

The 16th New York remained in service until May 22, 1863, serving with both the I and VI Corps in the Army of the Potomac. Following their losses on the Peninsula, the New Yorkers also suffered heavily at Crampton's Gap during the Antietam campaign and at Salem Church in the Chancellorsville campaign.

Low-crowned straw hat worn by James J. Lampton of Company K
(Columbus Riflemen), 13th Mississippi Regiment. Accustomed to
wearing such hats during civilian life in the steamy climes,
Southerners frequently employed this ample headgear in military
service. CONFEDERATE MEMORIAL HALL, CLAUDE LEVET PHOTOGRAPH.

Leather leggings such as this pair worn by a soldier of the 26th Massachusetts
Volunteers often proved hot and uncomfortable on campaign. By the summer of
1862, few were seen in either army. TROIANI COLLECTION.

New York State uniform jacket worn by Sgt. Rollin B. Truesdell
of the 27th Regiment. With an exterior breast pocket, state seal
buttons, and simple light blue piping around the collar and
shoulder straps, these jackets were widely issued from 1861 until
about mid-1863. TROIANI COLLECTION.

Early-war-style officer's frock coat worn by Capt. J. B. Turner of Mile's Legion (Louisiana) when mortally wounded at Plain's Store on May 20, 1863, during the opening of the Port Hudson campaign. The coat is adorned with black herringbone braid on the front and gold on the black collar and cuffs. It was brought back by a Union officer and became part of the celebrated A. E. Brooks's Collection in 1899. WILLIAM BRAYTON COLLECTION.

ILLUSTRATED CATALOGUE: A. E. BROOKS'S COLLECTION OF ANTIQUE GUNS, PISTOLS, ETC. HARTFORD, CONN. (HARTFORD: CASE, LOCKWOOD & BRAINARD, 1899), 180–82.

One of the soldier's most vital necessities on the march was the haversack in which he carried rations. Although many types were used, the standard tarred Federal-issue version shown here was by far the most prevalent. TROIANI COLLECTION.

19TH TENNESSEE INFANTRY, C.S.A., APRIL 1862

The 19th Tennessee Infantry was composed of companies from all over eastern Tennessee. Although Union sentiment was strong in this part of the state, this Confederate regiment was raised and organized with little trouble in May and June 1861. The various companies were assembled at Knoxville and entered Confederate service on August 15. Although the regiment received ample supplies of uniforms and equipment in September and October, the armament left something to be desired, with most of the men receiving obsolete flintlock muskets.

As luck would have it, the regiment's first major engagement at Fishing Creek, Kentucky, on January 19, 1862, was under conditions that were unsuited to the arms they carried. One officer remembered that "the rain poured down so they [the flintlocks] would not fire at all. Several of the men after trying repeatedly to fire, just broke their guns over a fence or around a tree, and went off in disgust." The battle was a disaster for the Confederates. A night retreat forced them to abandon a large amount of equipment and supplies. The command, which included the 19th Tennessee, fell back to Nashville.

During the next two months, the 19th was reissued needed uniform items, including frock coats and caps, from the Nashville Quartermaster Depot. Many of the flintlock muskets were exchanged for percussion muskets and a few for Mississippi rifles. Within a few weeks, those who still carried the flintlocks had ample opportunity to exchange them for more modern arms on the bloody field of Shiloh.

On the morning of April 6, 1862, the Tennesseans were in the ranks of the Confederate army commanded by Albert Sidney Johnston near Shiloh Church as part of Gen. John C. Breckinridge's Division. Before the attack on the unsuspecting Union camps, the 19th was detached and moved to the extreme right of the Confederate line. From here, they became part of the afternoon attack on the Union left. Casualties were high, possibly as many as 25 percent killed and wounded, but the men of the 19th Tennessee showed clearly the courage that would carry them through the remainder of the war. Those that remained in 1865 surrendered with Gen. Joseph E. Johnston's Confederate army in North Carolina.

WILLIAM RODEN

FIRE ON CAROLINE STREET

The men of the 20th Massachusetts, known as the "Harvard Regiment" for the number of Harvard students and graduates in its ranks, engaged in a vicious house-to-house fight as they cleared Confederate soldiers from Fredericksburg, Virginia, on December 11, 1862. The 20th had crossed the Rappahannock River as one of the regiments of Hall's Brigade, Howard's Division, in makeshift "assault" boats in the first bridgehead landing under fire in American history.

Their struggle in the streets of the old colonial town was vicious. As they pushed into Fredericksburg, the men of the 20th found Confederates lodged in its shell-battered and partially wrecked homes and stores. It took the remainder of the day to push the stubborn defenders out of the town and into what proved to be even stronger defenses. The next day, the Harvard Regiment participated in the assault on Marye's Heights. On that day, the 20th could not drive the Southern soldiers from their position, and in two days of fighting, its total casualties numbered 200 killed or wounded.

The 20th was a smart regiment. The men kept their issue uniforms in good order, and on this cold day, they covered their flannel sack coats and sky blue kersey trousers with distinctive gray overcoats. They wore these state-issued overcoats with pride, for their governor, John Andrews, had procured them especially for his state's troops. The regiment was also distinguished by red blankets rolled atop their knapsacks, adding a touch of color, unlike the drab, gray Federal blankets. As a show of regimental pride, many men placed the numeral 20 and the abbreviation "MASS" on the tops of their forage caps. The regiment's Enfield rifle muskets were clean and in good order, and the men of the 20th put them to good use in Fredericksburg on December 11 and 12, 1862.

Federal officer's McDowell pattern forage cap, with downward cast visor and scarlet diamond badge of the III Army Corps. Also ornamented with small, false-embroidered stamped silver-plated numbers, which designate it as having belonged to an officer of the 17th Maine Volunteers. TROIANI COLLECTION.

Black Federal overcoat worn by Pvt. David Dazell of the 49th Massachusetts Volunteers. Early in the war, Northern contractors were allowed to supply overcoats of other than the regulation sky blue. They were not liked in the 49th, as reported in the November 22, 1862, Boston Daily Advertiser: "Through the efforts of Col. Bartlett, the miserable black overcoats have been exchanged, and the regiment will soon receive the serviceable light blue overcoats similar to those of the 51st." TROIANI COLLECTION.

Advertised as "Canvass Zouave Army Shoes!" in a Hartford, Connecticut, newspaper during the summer of 1862, these distinctive shoes proved popular with Union troops in both the Eastern and Western Theaters of war. The Allyn House Boot and Shoe Store pronounced, "For marching; they are the best Shoe made, combining comfort and economy. . . . Volunteers attended to first. Drafted men can call after the 15th inst." Volunteer Edgar S. Yergason of the 22nd Connecticut, original owner of the pictured pair, was among those not obliged to wait until the fifteenth to purchase his Zouave shoes. TROIANI COLLECTION.

HARTFORD DAILY COURANT, AUGUST 2 AND 18, 1862.

12TH TENNESSEE REGIMENT

The 12th Tennessee Infantry Regiment, the majority of its companies recruited in Gibson County, was organized into state service on June 3, 1861, at Jackson, Tennessee. In September, the regiment was ordered to Columbus, Kentucky, on the Mississippi River, as part of the garrison. Surviving quartermaster documents for the 12th Tennessee show that substantial amounts of clothing were issued during October and November 1861, including overcoats, both flannel and cotton shirts, socks, blankets, boots and shoes, pants, hats, caps, and frock coats.

A description from Columbus, Kentucky, printed in the October 30, 1861, *New York Herald* said of the Confederate soldiers that "half were uniformed . . . while balance had an Army cap, coat, pants with a stripe or military mark of some kind, and the rest simply some ordinary [civilian] costume."

Several photographs of soldiers from the 12th Tennessee, as well as the 3rd, 6th, 22nd, 29th, 31st, and 55th Tennessee Battalions, show frock coats of similar style and cut. These are eight- or nine-button single-breasted frocks, with distinctive pointed cuffs that have three buttons. The fabrics and facings are of several different colors, the coats of a dark blue-gray or gray satinette or jean cloth, with facings of light blue, black, or red.

An August 31, 1861 article, in the *Nashville Union and American* stated that the Quartermaster Department was making 2,000 garments per day and had on hand 14,000 suits of clothing. In Memphis, a similar manufacturing depot employed 300 women making up piecework clothing for the Tennessee soldiers. In April and May 1861, to provide uniforms for the Tennessee Volunteers, the Tennessee State and Financial Board had purchased some 30,000 yards of gray satinette material; 25,000 yards of mixed red, gray, and blue flannel cloth; Kentucky jean cloth; 25,000 yards of red flannel; and metal coat buttons.

Ads were run in the Nashville papers for six or eight practical tailors to cut volunteer uniforms by pattern. In September 1861, the operations and supplies of the Tennessee State Quartermaster Department were transferred to the Confederate government. In addition to Tennessee soldiers, the Memphis and Nashville Depots were to also supply clothing to the troops from Kentucky, Missouri, and Arkansas. By the fall of 1861, Nashville was the primary supply center for the Confederate armies in the Western Department No. 2 and those in faraway Virginia.

Nashville was evacuated in February 1862, following the battle and capture of Fort Donelson. Some $5 million of much-needed quartermaster goods were abandoned or destroyed in what has been called the Nashville Panic. It appears that the Tennessee pattern frock coat was also lost to the enemy. Instead, the less expensive jacket was now manufactured and issued to the soldiers of the Confederacy.

The 12th Tennessee was consolidated with the 22nd Tennessee Infantry in June 1862 and with the 47th Tennessee Infantry in October of that year. The regiment's proud history began with the battle of Belmont, where it, along with the rest of Col. Robert Russell's Brigade, bore the first shock of the Federal attack. Battle honors include some of the bloodiest fighting of the war—Shiloh, Richmond (Kentucky), and Murfreesboro, where the 12th suffered 164 casualties out of 322 engaged, a staggering 50 percent casualty rate.

The 12th Tennessee served on in the Western Theater of the war until paroled at Greensboro, North Carolina, in May 1865. At the surrender, there remained a total of only fifty officers and men of the consolidated 12th, 22nd, and 47th Tennessee Regiments.

Confederate enlisted man's double-breasted frock coat made of gray-brown jean cloth. The inscription "L.S. 2nd Ala Vols" is marked inside the sleeve. The buttons are covered with black cloth and probably were added after the war's end when Confederate insignia were banned from public display. MIDDLESEX COUNTY HISTORICAL SOCIETY.

Gray satinette frock coat with black binding worn by Pvt. Joseph Ellison Adger, a member of Company A (Washington Light Infantry), 25th Regiment of South Carolina Infantry. Adger frugally retained this coat when promoted to captain in April 1862, adding the appropriate gold tape to the collar. COLLECTION OF THE CHARLESTON (SOUTH CAROLINA) MUSEUM.

Pair of woven cotton butternut trousers worn by Pvt. James A. McKinstry of Company D, 42nd Alabama. According to family tradition, they were worn by him at the assault on Battery Robinett, Corinth, Mississippi, on October 3, 1862. COURTESY JAMES VANCE.

BURNSIDE'S BRIDGE

On September 17, 1862, two Union infantry regiments forced the crossing of a narrow stone bridge that spanned Antietam Creek. These regiments, one from New York and one from Pennsylvania, both bore the regimental number 51. First to cross were the Pennsylvanians, their three regimental colors leading the way. Facing them were 400 Confederates of the 2nd and 20th Georgia Regiments, determined to exact a high toll in Yankee blood as the price of passage. There was no unique color or flash to the uniform of the 51st Pennsylvania. Brigade quartermaster records show issue of the standard fatigue blouse and forage cap. They were armed with the Enfield rifle musket.

The men had seen action just a month before at Second Manassas, where they had the misfortune of having left their knapsacks stacked under guard, only to lose them when forced to leave the field by a different route. Except for a small amount of clothing intended for another regiment, which they found at Centerville, Virginia, they would have no new issue until late September. On September 28, the regiment received a new stand of colors from friends in Norristown, Pennsylvania, and on October 5, a new individual button-together shelter tent known officially as the *tente d'abri,* which would soon become well known to Union soldiers.

As part of the IX Army Corps, commanded by Maj. Gen. Ambrose Burnside, the 51st Pennsylvania saw service in both theaters of the war. Its men fought on until the end, sustaining a total of 177 killed and mortally wounded. But despite all the hard fighting and campaigns, they would forever be linked to the few brave minutes of their desperate charge across the stone bridge at Antietam, ever after known as Burnside's Bridge.

NATIONAL CIVIL WAR MUSEUM, HARRISBURG, PENNSYLVANIA

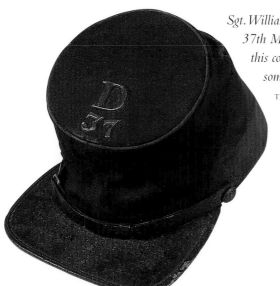

Sgt. William H. Shaw of Company D, 37th Massachusetts Volunteers, purchased this commercial-grade forage cap for himself sometime between 1862 and 1865. TROIANI COLLECTION.

A pair of manufactured Federal sky blue kersey enlisted man's trousers. These were made by the hundreds of thousands by the government and private contractors throughout the war. This pair has a one-and-a-half-inch-wide dark blue stripe denoting a sergeant of infantry, which was added by the soldier himself. TROIANI COLLECTION.

The men of Congressman (Col.) Charles H. Van Wyck's 56th New York Volunteer Infantry had a unique description—Xth Legion—to display on their Model 1853/1855 knapsacks. The regiment was considered a legion because when it was formed, it had infantry, artillery, rifle, and cavalry companies in one unit. The name derived from the fact that Van Wyck represented the Tenth District of New York. WEST POINT MUSEUM.

PRIVATE, 5TH NEW JERSEY INFANTRY, MAY 1863

In the spring of 1863, as the Army of the Potomac began to prepare for the coming campaign, each regiment was ordered to box surplus clothing for storage until needed again the following winter. Because of their weight, blankets and greatcoats were generally included in the items stored. Brigade commanders often decided which uniform items would be worn and which stored. Although most regiments of the army elected to wear the four-button fatigue blouse, the men of the 3rd Brigade, 2nd Division, III Corps, consisting of the 5th, 6th, 7th, and 8th New Jersey, as well as the 115th Pennsylvania and 2nd New Hampshire commanded by Col. George C. Burling, either elected to or were ordered to wear the dress frock coat. During this same period, on February 19, 1863, the III Corps received a general order that the infantry would be issued white canvas or leather leggings by the Quartermaster Department. Also during this time of preparation for battle, the famous corps identifying badges were adopted by the Army of the Potomac. The 2nd Division, III Corps, would wear a white diamond attached to the forage cap.

The soldier illustrated here represents the 5th New Jersey as it appeared just before the battle of Chancellorsville. He is armed with a .54-caliber Austrian Lorenz rifle musket. His uniform is army regulation, and he will wear it throughout the coming campaign, which will include the battle at Chancellorsville and the march to and battle of Gettysburg. At Gettysburg, the 5th New Jersey would be sent forward as skirmishers west of the Emmitsburg Road and on July 2 would find themselves temporarily trapped between the Union and Confederate lines, where they would take numerous casualties.

JOSEPH STAHL

The regiment served in the III Corps until March 1864, when they were assigned to the 3rd Division of the II Corps. Those who did not reenlist were mustered out the following November. During its service, the 5th New Jersey lost 12 officers and 126 enlisted men, killed and mortally wounded.

First Sgt. Enoch Whittemore of Company I, 5th Maine Volunteers, may have worn this jacket when he received his third gunshot wound of the war at Spotsylvania, Virginia, on May 10, 1864. Whittemore had sported an officers'-quality 1st Division, VI Corps, badge on the breast of his jacket, a common practice of the time, as evidenced in contemporary photographs. TROIANI COLLECTION.

Although enlisted men were not authorized to wear a vest, many did so during their term of service. This example was made from the same rough sky blue kersey used for trousers and overcoats. NELSONIAN INSTITUTE.

In early 1862, many units of the Army of the Potomac received canvas leggings of this pattern, including the regiments composing the famed Iron Brigade. The leggings were heavily used at first, but they quickly became unpopular and were not widely worn after early 1863, although they continued to be issued sporadically through 1864. This pair was issued to Pvt. James Boisbrun of Company A, 115th Pennsylvania Volunteers. TROIANI COLLECTION.

14TH MISSISSIPPI INFANTRY, FORT DONELSON, TENNESSEE, FEBRUARY 18, 1863

As the officers and men of the 14th Mississippi began their two-mile walk from the train station to the Camp Douglas Prison Camp in Chicago, a soldier in Company B of that regiment remarked that his comrades made for a "motley looking set." As he described it, "We had all our cooking utensils with us, camp kettles, skillets, ovens, frying pans, coffee pots, tin pans, tin cups and plates. We had them on our heads, on our backs, swinging from our sides, and in our hands. Some of the boys were bareheaded, some had hats and caps with no brims . . . we were quite a show!" According to a reporter for the *Chicago Tribune* who witnessed the arrival of this first group of Confederate prisoners:

Such a thing as uniformity in dress was impossible to find, as there were no two dressed alike. Butternut colored breeches, walnut dyed jeans greatly predominated. Most of the pants were ornamented by a broad, black stripe down the outer seam, sometimes of velvet, but mostly of cloth or serge. Shirts and drawers are all of the coarsest description. Hats and caps were diversified, yet they had a uniform cap— gray with black band. For protection against the chilling wind, the soldiers used a conglomeration of overcoats, blankets, quilts, buffalo robes, and pieces of carpeting of all colors and figures. The carpet coats are made by putting a puckering string in the edge of a piece of carpeting, and gathering it around the edge. Their officers could not be distinguished from the privates, although some had a regular gray uniform and others the Army blue, the only difference a great profusion of gold lace. Many of the soldiers carried bags [carpet sacks] of all colors, and were dressed in butternut jeans and white cotton [osnaburg] overcoats. All appeared rough and hard.

The nonuniform appearance of the early- to midwar Confederate soldiers was a direct result of goods being collected and distributed in two clothing drives, as the Quartermaster Department was unable to provide clothing for an army of 200,000 men until later in the war. In a show of unequaled patriotism by the fair women of the South, their tender hands spun and dyed the jean cloth for uniforms and sewed and collected most of the garments worn by the Fort Donelson garrison. This they accomplished under two "great appeals" for warm winter clothing, blankets, and shoes. The appeals were officially government sponsored, with the full support of the Quartermaster Department, which promised to provide transportation of the goods. These drives were the primary source of clothing for all the armies of the South during the fall and winter of 1861–62 and 1862–63. The bulk of the uniforms collected were homespun jeans, gathered up and sent to state collection points as donations or traded for Confederate bonds.

During the four-day siege and battles of Fort Donelson, February 12–16, 1862, the 14th Mississippi Infantry lost 17 killed, 85 wounded, and 10 missing out of 650 engaged. On February 15, the 14th Mississippi was part of the Confederate counterattack to open the way for a retreat or a Federal rout. Twice that day, the 14th Mississippi was ordered to make a bayonet charge to break the Yankee line. It succeeded, only to be ordered back to its trenches and surrendered.

The 14th was exchanged on August 27, 1862, after spending six long months in a prisoner-of-war camp in Chicago. The regiment went on to fight in some of the bloodiest battles of the Western Theater, serving gallantly at Vicksburg, and in the Atlanta campaign and Hood's Nashville campaign, finally ending its service in North Carolina in April 1865.

Light-colored jean cloth Confederate trousers typical of those produced in penitentiary workshops. This pair was used by Nathan Tisdale of Company A, 30th Louisiana Infantry, who served at Meridian, Mississippi, from early 1862 until his parole on May 14, 1865. CONFEDERATE MEMORIAL HALL, CLAUDE LEVET PHOTOGRAPH.

Confederate soldier's rubberized rain hat, taken as a trophy by a Union soldier from the battlefield of Corinth, Mississippi, in May 1862. Products of the India Rubber Company, waterproof garments such as this were used by both sides. TROIANI COLLECTION.

Typical Confederate tin drum canteen, with a Federal musket sling as a shoulder strap. This specimen was captured at Gettysburg by George H. Sunderlin from Vermont, who survived the fighting to bring home this memento. TROIANI COLLECTION.

13TH PENNSYLVANIA RESERVES

In early April 1861, Thomas L. Kane, an active abolitionist, applied to Pennsylvania governor Andrew G. Curtin for permission to raise companies of cavalry for the war. Since no cavalry was wanted, Kane decided instead to raise a regiment of riflemen from rural Pennsylvanians "accustomed to handling guns . . . and possessed of strong and dogged physiques through their outdoor experiences." Kane got exactly what he wanted, and the volunteers rushed to service, armed with their own rifles. While Kane's recruits were signing up, James Landregan of the Macon County Rifles spied a deer's hide hanging in a butcher shop opposite the recruiting office. He cut off the tail and placed it on his cap, thus giving birth to the regimental insignia and nickname of Bucktails.

The Bucktails were not at all happy to find the government offering them flintlock conversion smoothbore muskets to replace their personal rifles, but in August 1861, they received Enfield and Springfield rifle muskets, which somewhat placated the men. Known also as the 42nd Regiment, Pennsylvania Volunteer Infantry, the Bucktails never wore a special uniform. Initially they were issued standard uniforms of blouses, caps, and dark blue trousers. In Harrisburg, late in July, "Letters to be placed on the men's caps were obtained, as were also blue overcoats, cotton-flannel drawers and other necessary clothing." Thus equipped, the men of the 13th Reserves went to war. They were, however, immediately identifiable by the bucktails and strips of deerhide that they continued to wear on their caps, hats, and even their flagstaffs throughout the war.

By the summer of 1862, the Bucktails had established their reputation but had suffered losses. Two new regiments of Bucktails were raised—the 149th and 150th Pennsylvania—to create a Bucktail Brigade. Much to the initial chagrin of the 13th, the new, unproven regiments were allowed to wear the cherished fur emblem of the original regiment. The original Bucktails, however, were recognized in August 1862 with the issuance of double-set trigger Sharps M1859

NATHAN EDELSTEIN

breech-loading rifles. They used these new weapons with great effect at Gettysburg, in a hot struggle in the woods near that battle's famed Wheatfield. There the regiment's new twenty-three-year-old colonel, Charles Frederick Taylor, was killed while in the front lines with his men. A Medal of Honor was awarded to Sgt. James B. Thompson for capturing the flag of the 15th Georgia at this battle.

The 13th fought on, greatly reduced in numbers, if not in spirit, through the first campaigns with Grant in 1864. In June 1864, the original regiment of Bucktails was mustered out of service. They left an indelible record of valor.

Pair of forage caps worn by Federal soldiers of the 5th Maine and 119th Pennsylvania Volunteers. Both bear the Greek cross of the 1st Division, VI Army Corps. TROIANI COLLECTION.

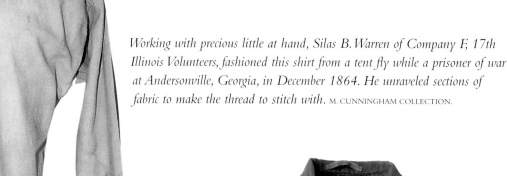

Working with precious little at hand, Silas B. Warren of Company F, 17th Illinois Volunteers, fashioned this shirt from a tent fly while a prisoner of war at Andersonville, Georgia, in December 1864. He unraveled sections of fabric to make the thread to stitch with. M. CUNNINGHAM COLLECTION.

Pvt. Edgar S. Yergason of Company A, 22nd Connecticut Volunteers, favored superior garments than those issued to him by the army. In many regiments, the colonel showed indifference to privately purchased items by his men such as this officers'-quality sack coat. In his quest to achieve comfort, Private Yergason reduced the buttons on the front of his coat from four to two. TROIANI COLLECTION.

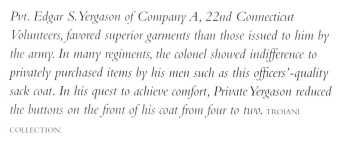

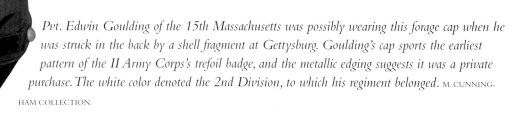

Pvt. Edwin Goulding of the 15th Massachusetts was possibly wearing this forage cap when he was struck in the back by a shell fragment at Gettysburg. Goulding's cap sports the earliest pattern of the II Army Corps's trefoil badge, and the metallic edging suggests it was a private purchase. The white color denoted the 2nd Division, to which his regiment belonged. M. CUNNINGHAM COLLECTION.

THE IRON BRIGADE

As the Union I Army Corps fell back toward the town of Gettysburg on July 1, 1863, the 24th Michigan Infantry turned to fight a desperate rearguard action near the Lutheran Seminary. The regiment had arrived on the field early in the day with the rest of the famed Iron Brigade and had been heavily engaged ever since. Now, with several color-bearers down, the regiment's colonel, Henry A. Morrow, defiantly raised the regimental colors.

The 24th Michigan Infantry had been the last regiment to join the Army of the Potomac's famed Iron Brigade, arriving in October 1862. It was also the last to trade its forage caps for the black army dress hats that had become the symbol of the rest of the brigade, not receiving them until May 27, 1863. These hats now bore the recently adopted corps badge of the 1st Division, I Corps, a red cloth disk, along with the brass numerals and letters dictated by army regulations. Although the men of the 24th had sent their greatcoats and excess clothing to storage before the summer campaign, most had elected to retain and wear their infantry dress coats. Wearing these, along with knapsacks or bedrolls—which experience had shown must be worn into battle, as few such items that were removed and stacked were ever recovered—made hot work even hotter.

Regulation infantry officer's Hardee hat. The embroidered insignia was fastened by cloth or leather strips run through loops on the reverse, allowing military goods dealers to furnish, within minutes, hats with the required branch of service emblems. TROIANI COLLECTION.

Federal army-issue blanket manufactured under contract by Robert Beattie & Son of Little Falls, New Jersey, and marked "R B & Son." The Beattie firm had contracts for approximately 140,000 blankets between 1862 and 1865. This example was used by Lt. George W. Harper of the 102nd Pennsylvania Volunteers, who had his initials and the date "1863" woven into the stripe. TROIANI COLLECTION.

Short, doubled-breasted roundabout with rank shown on the sleeves worn by Lt. Col. Edward L. Gaul of the 159th New York Volunteers. The similarity in cut to a naval undress jacket is explained by the fact that Gaul had served in the U.S. Navy earlier in the war and obviously favored the style. TROIANI COLLECTION.

21ST OHIO VOLUNTEER INFANTRY, CORPORAL, COMPANY C, SEPTEMBER 1863

The uniform of the 21st Ohio in 1863 was typical of that worn by Federal troops serving in the Western Theater of the war. The campaigns of the winter and early spring had taken their toll on the uniforms of the regiment, and it was issued new ones in August. This uniform had none of the flash or color of the Zouave. Every item from head to toe had a practical value and was standard issue, as received from one of the two Western quartermaster depots. This soldier's hat is unadorned, and his coat is the plain fatigue blouse of a fighting man ready for action. The only bit of regulation flash present is the round brass plate bearing a U.S. eagle on the sling holding his cartridge box at his side. Even this eventually was dispensed with as the men moved in combat.

If the uniform of the 21st can be considered typical, the arms they carried were anything but commonplace. Company C, like most of the 21st Ohio, was armed with the deadly .56-caliber, five-shot Colt revolving rifle, which it received in a shipment from Washington on May 26, 1863. Many, if not most, of the rifles carried by the regiment had been turned in by the famed 2nd Regiment U. S. Sharpshooters serving in Virginia, who disliked the complicated mechanism. As with other Eastern discards, the rifles were sent west where, in the hands of the farm boys and mechanics of the Buckeye State, they soon proved their worth. On September 20, at the bloody battle of Chickamauga, the men of the 21st were ordered to hold a position on Horseshoe Ridge, and hold it they did. Their rapid-firing Colts repulsed repeated Confederate charges and inflicted heavy losses on the enemy. Finally, when the special ammunition required to load the rifles was exhausted, they fixed bayonets and continued to fight. During this single day's fight, the 21st Ohio, with their rapid-firing Colts, expended over 43,000 rounds of ammunition.

Not withstanding their heroic stand, the regiment lost a

number of men captured by Confederate troops of Gen. James Longstreet's command, who, according to the regimental historian of the 21st, "were wearing new uniforms which at a distance in the smoke and dusk of the evening, looked very much as our own."

The remaining men of the 21st Ohio continued to serve and fight with the XIV Corps and the Army of the Cumberland in the Atlanta campaign and through the Carolinas. They were mustered out on July 25, 1865.

TOWARD THE ANGLE

The battle of Gettysburg will forever be remembered as one of the defining engagements of the Civil War. On July 3, 1863, with two days of indecisive battle behind him, Gen. Robert E. Lee, commanding the Confederate army, attempted to break the Federal line in its center. To accomplish this, he ordered an assault by three divisions of infantry totaling nearly 12,000 men, under the overall command of Gen. George E. Pickett. It was a fateful decision that gained the Southern army nothing but glory and cost the lives of many of its finest officers and men.

Among those who would lead and not return were Brig. Gen. Richard Brooke Garnett, commanding one brigade of five Virginia regiments, and Brig. Gen. Lewis Addison Armistead, in command of another five regiments of Virginians. As they moved forward, the men of these regiments presented a picture that sharply contrasted with the image of the poorly uniformed and supplied Confederate soldier. Garnett was wearing a fine new gray uniform. In May and June 1863, prior to leaving Virginia, the men of the Army of Northern Virginia who needed new uniform items had received replacements. For the infantry, these replacements included jackets and caps, many trimmed in infantry blue, as well as trousers, shirts, and underwear from the Richmond Depot, and the vital commodity of shoes. Although the depot-produced uniforms were of a high quality, the character of the shoes varied depending on the source and materials available. The fortunate received footwear of English manufacture, which buckled rather than tied. In the opinion of one Federal officer who saw them, they were "the best I have seen for Army use."

Although some Confederates were issued and carried knapsacks, many preferred what the army termed "light marching order"—a rolled blanket containing a few personal items and a change of underwear, slung over the shoulder. Like their Yankee counterparts, the Southern soldiers had learned by experience that stacking or leaving their belongings behind when going into battle usually meant they would never see them again.

A pair of English-manufactured shoes run through the blockade for the Confederacy. In 1863, a Federal quartermaster examining this type of shoe described it as "made of well tanned leather very well curried, but not blacked the grain side[,] is as usual high in the ankle and confined by straps and buckle instead of string." He then pronounced them "the best I have seen for Army use." TROIANI COLLECTION.

NATIONAL ARCHIVES, RECORD GROUP 92, ENTRY 999, LE DUC LETTER, LIEUTENANT COLONEL AND CHIEF QUARTERMASTER, XI CORPS.

DR. COYLE S. CONNOLLY

This cadet gray Confederate kepi of the style produced at the Richmond Depot, with painted fabric visor, was brought home as a war trophy by a Union soldier. COLLECTION OF NEW YORK STATE DIVISION OF MILITARY AND NAVAL AFFAIRS.

THE TEXAS BRIGADE, 1863

One of the fabled units of the Confederate army of Northern Virginia, the Texas Brigade, lived up to the hard-fighting reputation it gained on battlefields from Virginia to Pennsylvania. This brigade consisted of the 1st, 4th, and 5th Texas Infantry, along with the 3rd Arkansas Infantry. By 1863, after two years of campaigning, the uniforms worn by the brigade were much the same as those in general use in the Eastern Confederate army. To assure as ample a supply as possible, each of the regiments of this brigade maintained its own depot in Richmond, where surplus clothing was stored until needed. Prior to the summer campaign of 1863, each regiment had all needed clothing items supplied. The campaign that led to the monumental battle at Gettysburg, Pennsylvania, took its toll on both uniforms and equipment for the Texas Brigade. Most, if not all, items were resupplied after the brigade returned to Virginia, before it left again with the Confederate First Corps to temporarily bolster the sagging fortunes of the Confederate Army of Tennessee.

The four soldiers on the previous page represent, from left to right, the 1st, 5th, and 4th Texas, as well as a musician of the 3rd Arkansas. They stand together just prior to the attack on the Federal left flank at Devil's Den on July 2, 1863.

During the first months of 1863, the 4th Texas had received an extensive issue of clothing, which included caps with rain covers. The soldier of the 1st Regiment has removed the frock coat he was issued earlier in the year. The noncommissioned officer of the 5th carries the short Enfield rifle with saber bayonet that he received in 1861. The arms carried by the brigade varied, but with the exception of the 1st Texas, they consisted mainly of .57- or .58-caliber rifle muskets. The men of the 1st received and carried a mixture of .69-caliber smoothbore muskets and rifle muskets, with the smoothbores continuing in service well into 1864.

While the brigade was in the Department of Tennessee in early 1864, and away from its clothing supply from the regimental depots in Richmond, it was necessary to detail several shoemakers from the 4th Texas to manufacture shoes and boots from leather obtained by the regimental quartermaster. During this time, for the 4th Texas alone, the detailed men manufactured 259 pairs of shoes and 22 pairs of boots. Along with its corps, the Texas Brigade returned east in time for the fateful campaigns of 1864 and the spring of 1865.

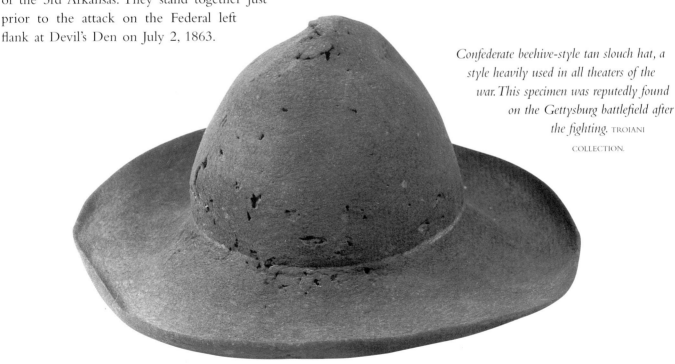

Confederate beehive-style tan slouch hat, a style heavily used in all theaters of the war. This specimen was reputedly found on the Gettysburg battlefield after the fighting. TROIANI

COLLECTION.

BARKSDALE'S CHARGE

On July 2, 1863, Confederate general William Barksdale and his four Mississippi regiments of infantry—the 13th, 17th, 18th, and 21st—advanced upon Federal artillery and infantry along Emmitsburg Road near the Peach Orchard. Barksdale's men were part of the overall assault of Longstreet's Corps on that hot and sunny afternoon. It was an attack that Robert E. Lee hoped would sweep the opposing Army of the Potomac from Gettysburg. If successful, it could decide the course of the war.

The 1,500 men of Barksdale's units were noted as "well shod and efficiently clothed" by Lt. Col. Arthur Fremantle, a British Army observer accompanying Lee's army. Their accoutrements included Union army knapsacks captured at the battles of Second Manassas and Chancellorsville, many of which still bore the names of the regiments to whom they had belonged. Uniformed in gray jackets, often worn with captured Federal blue trousers, Barksdale's men had a variety of headgear, from civilian brimmed hats to jaunty regulation kepis of gray and blue.

On the other side, however, there was greater uniformity, and as the advance neared the Sherfy farmhouse and barn just west of the Emmitsburg Road, the distinctive uniforms of the 114th Pennsylvania Volunteer Infantry became apparent. A Zouave unit, the 114th wore uniforms of dark blue and red with red fezzes, some wrapped in white turbans, but all with yellow tassels. The haughty Englishman, Fremantle, described them as "poor imitations" of the French Zouave garb, but the 114th uniforms were actually well made and attractive, with light blue cuffs adorning the red-trimmed jackets.

Barksdale's gray smashed into the blue-and-red lines and sent them reeling, forcing the Rhode Island artillerymen to limber their guns in hasty withdrawal. Pennsylvania regiments in standard blue were also forced back, and the Mississippi regiments plunged forward through the Peach Orchard, pushing on to further combat that would see hundreds of soldiers, as well as the valiant Barksdale, fall as the Union lines ultimately held to fight another day.

Painted infantry drum used by Edwin S. Sutch, drummer of Company C, 138th Pennsylvania Volunteers. This example is unusual in having a large VI Corps badge incorporated within a striking motif on its front. C. PAUL LOANE COLLECTION.

1ST SOUTH CAROLINA VOLUNTEER INFANTRY, U.S. COLORED TROOPS

Aside from its status as one of the first regiments of African-American troops formed, the 1st South Carolina was also one of the only regiments, black or white, to see service before being officially recognized as a military unit. The 1st had been on an expedition along the coasts of Georgia and Florida in November 1862. Its first real service as a regiment came in a weeklong expedition up the St. Mary's River on the Georgia-Florida border in January 1863. It was here, at Township, Florida, that the 1st saw its first action in a skirmish with Confederate cavalry. The men of the new black regiment fought well and received praise in the Northern press. In February 1864, the regiment was redesigned the 33rd Regiment U.S. Colored Infantry. It continued to serve in the area of South Carolina, Georgia, and Florida until mustered out on January 31, 1866.

The soldiers depicted here wear the first uniform issued to the 1st South Carolina. Except for the red trousers, it is the regulation U.S. Army pattern. The trousers were similar to those worn by the French Army and were probably felt to be an inducement to enlist. Such inducement was not needed, and the different color made the men of the regiment feel that they were being set apart from the white regiments, who all wore the regulation sky blue. Col. Thomas Wentworth Higginson petitioned Gen. David Hunter to have a second issue of trousers, and by mid-February 1863, the blue trousers had been received. Throughout 1863, at least five types of firearms were carried by the 1st South Carolina. These were a mixed lot of Springfields and Enfields, as well as .69-caliber foreign-made arms of different types. By January 1864, these had all been replaced with the latest Springfield rifle muskets. At last the physical hurdles had been overcome. There were many more social hurdles, however, some of which would far outlive the men of the 1st South Carolina Infantry.

WILLIAM GLADSTONE

27TH VIRGINIA INFANTRY, COLOR SERGEANT, DECEMBER 1862

By the winter of 1862, supply problems for the Confederate Army of Northern Virginia were beginning to stabilize. Although still relying on state issue and home supply, the Confederate Quartermaster Department in Richmond was now procuring uniforms in adequate numbers to clothe the army. Despite the fact that the quality and color of uniform items varied with the source of supply, the soldiers of this army were much better off than they had been just one year previously. At the same time, the Confederate arsenal, also in Richmond, was coming into full production of arms and ammunition. The Federal naval blockade of Southern ports, though an annoyance, was not yet a serious problem, and shortfalls in domestic production of both uniforms and arms were, to a great extent, compensated for by goods from Europe brought in by daring blockade runners. Regimental records of units such as the 27th Virginia Infantry show a slow but steady supply of all matériel needed to sustain a military organization on active campaign.

In many ways, the 27th Virginia was typical of the first regiments raised for Confederate service in the early months of the war. The regiment was raised in May 1861 and, along with the 2nd, 4th, 5th, and 33rd Virginia Infantry Regiments, formed a brigade that was initially commanded by Brig. Gen. Thomas J. "Stonewall" Jackson. Although Jackson soon went on to higher command, the regiments remained together to gain fame and glory as the hard-fighting Stonewall Brigade.

The color sergeant shown here holds one of the flags carried by the 27th Virginia during its years of service. This flag, along with its Confederate-issue octagonal staff, was received by the regiment on August 4, 1862. The soldier's overcoat is of English manufacture. Along with English shirts, these overcoats were welcome additions to the men's uniforms as the cold Virginia winter approached. Several pairs of black trousers made of the wool-cotton material known as cassimere were issued to every company of the 27th Virginia in October 1862. Similar trousers were issued on a periodic basis to Confederate troops throughout the war. The color sergeant's woolen jacket is a product of the Richmond Depot, as are his shoes. The brass frame buckle on his belt is typical of those commonly issued to the Army of Northern Virginia. Hats and caps both appear in the records of issue to the 27th. The chevrons to indicate the rank of this sergeant are hidden under the coat he wears, but the stature of those chosen to carry the regimental colors in Civil War regiments was such that all who served in the ranks would have known who he was. The fact that by the second winter of the war the regiments serving with this army were generally well supplied stands as a tribute to the ability and determination of the Confederacy to exist as a nation.

DAVID RANKIN, JR.

Regulation Federal infantry dress coat with light blue cord piping and worsted corporals' chevrons. This is only one of two known extant examples made by the firm of Rudensill & Lind of Lewistown, Pennsylvania, which had a government contract for 1,000 coats in 1862. This specimen was owned by Lemuel F. Liscom of Company A, 14th New Hampshire Volunteers. JOHN OCKERBLOOM COLLECTION.

Brass drum presented to Henry Galloway by the men of the 55th Massachusetts Volunteer Infantry, which was the second African-American regiment raised by the state. The band and drum corps was presented with instruments on Folly Island, South Carolina, in October 1864. "Nearly eleven hundred dollars were raised by the men, without aid or suggestion from the officers, to supply the Band and Drum Corps with Instruments." JOHN OCKERBLOOM COLLECTION.

CHARLES B. FOX, *RECORD OF SERVICE OF THE 55TH REGIMENT OF MASSACHUSETTS VOLUNTEERS* (1868; REPRINT, SALEM, N.H.: AYER, 1991), 3–4.

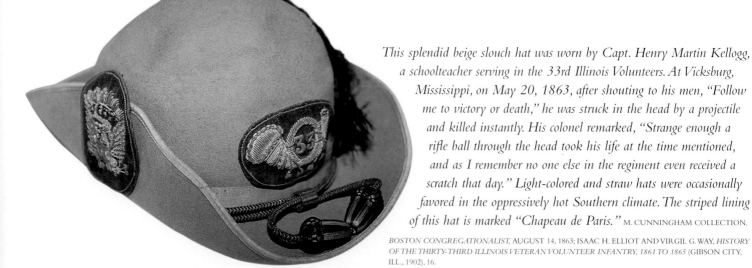

This splendid beige slouch hat was worn by Capt. Henry Martin Kellogg, a schoolteacher serving in the 33rd Illinois Volunteers. At Vicksburg, Mississippi, on May 20, 1863, after shouting to his men, "Follow me to victory or death," he was struck in the head by a projectile and killed instantly. His colonel remarked, "Strange enough a rifle ball through the head took his life at the time mentioned, and as I remember no one else in the regiment even received a scratch that day." Light-colored and straw hats were occasionally favored in the oppressively hot Southern climate. The striped lining of this hat is marked "Chapeau de Paris." M. CUNNINGHAM COLLECTION.

BOSTON CONGREGATIONALIST, AUGUST 14, 1863; ISAAC H. ELLIOT AND VIRGIL G. WAY, *HISTORY OF THE THIRTY-THIRD ILLINOIS VETERAN VOLUNTEER INFANTRY, 1861 TO 1865* (GIBSON CITY, ILL., 1902), 16.

Colonel of the Confederacy

When the first shots were fired in April 1861, little had been done to establish a regulation uniform for the Confederate army. A letter to the secretary of war dated April 30 asking what uniform had been adopted received the following reply: "Uniform is not yet established but that usually worn by our soldiers is a brave heart and steady arm." By June, uniform regulations had been published, with the uniform of officers bearing a strong resemblance to that of the Austrian Army. Rank would be indicated both on the collar of the coat and on the sleeve. Branch of service would be shown by the color of trim. Although numerous variations existed throughout the war, most officers followed at least the spirit of the regulations. Even with no indication of rank, however, the poise and dignity of the man depicted here could leave no doubt to any who saw him that he was in command. But battle authority must be instantly apparent to all. Three stars on the collar of his sky blue–trimmed coat, as well as a triple row of gold braid on each sleeve, would tell any soldier he was a colonel of infantry.

Confederate officer's brown leather waist belt with interlocking buckle and the letters "CS" in Old English. The original color was probably black. TROIANI COLLECTION.

Gold-taped Confederate officer's forage cap, with painted linen visor and sweatband. Layers of painted cloth provided a serviceable leather substitute for the hard-pressed Southern equipage producers.

M. CUNNINGHAM COLLECTION.

PRIVATE, 53RD GEORGIA INFANTRY, JULY 1863

The 53rd Georgia was organized in May 1862 and served until the final surrender in April 1865. The entire service of the regiment was with the famed First Corps of the Army of Northern Virginia. As part of Semmes's Brigade of McLaws's Division, the 53rd was part of the bloody fight for the Rose farm on July 2, 1863, at Gettysburg.

The Army of Northern Virginia, including Semmes's Brigade, had received several successive issues of new clothing during the spring and early summer of 1863. On May 20 and 21, each company of the 53rd received an issue that gave nearly every man a new outfit. Another issue in June supplemented the first. When the regiment began the march north, on the campaign that would lead them into Pennsylvania, each man was well clothed in the best the Confederacy had to offer.

The scarcity of leather in Southern depots caused the Confederate Ordnance Department to use substitute materials when they would serve the purpose. By 1863, cloth slings for cartridge boxes and cloth waist belts were often used. To serve this purpose, the material was folded several times to the proper width, and then securely stitched and tarred. The result was a very serviceable piece of equipment. One such sling, with its Confederate-made cartridge box, was found in a house in Cashtown, Pennsylvania, in the early 1960s and identified as having belonged to a soldier from a Georgia regiment.

Semmes's Brigade was in the process of obtaining rifle muskets during the first half of 1863. The soldier shown here is still armed with the M1842 smoothbore musket. By late in the year, however, most had been replaced.

L. JENSEN

The 1st Minnesota

The men of the 1st Minnesota Regiment of Volunteer Infantry had no distinctive or colorful uniform to make their regiment stand out on the battle line. The only items of dress that distinguished the 1st Minnesota were the white clover leaf, or trefoil, badge of the 2nd Division of the II Corps, Army of the Potomac, and the slouch hats (mixed with some forage caps) that Col. William Colvill described the regiment as wearing at Gettysburg. But clad in utilitarian dark blue flannel sack coats and sky blue kersey trousers, the 1st Minnesota proved it did not always take fancy uniforms to make good soldiers.

Adopted as a simple work garment for the Regular army in 1858, the sack coat became the most widely used piece of clothing in the quartermaster's inventory. All branches of service, and even a few officers, recognized the simple practicality of the garment. The sack coat had the added benefit of being cheap and easy to produce. With millions of them manufactured during the war years, sack coats did not disappear from the Federal supply system until the 1880s.

Still, it was the men inside the garments that mattered, and on July 2, 1863, when the commander of the II Corps, Winfield Scott Hancock, needed good men in a hurry, he was fortunate to find the 1st Minnesota. As survivors of the Confederate assault scurried to the safety of their lines, the men of the 1st could only watch the approaching juggernaut. Hancock ordered the regiment to attack as the advancing Confederate forces threatened to roll through the gap created in the Union lines by the retreat of other regiments. In a desperate and unbelievable effort, the 1st Minnesota withstood the Confederate onslaught, losing 82 percent of its men, with only 47 out of 262 left fit for combat. The regiment sacrificed itself to save the battle, proving that uniforms are only as good as the men who wear them.

Confederate .58-caliber cartridge box with painted canvas sling and oval, lead-backed brass Georgia state plate. Painted and unpainted canvas belts and straps were widely used in Southern accoutrement manufacture as leather resources dwindled. WILLIAM EQUITT COLLECTION.

Confederate-issue wooden canteen with leather shoulder strap, used by Daniel J. Foster of Company F, 35th Arkansas Regiment. Foster was captured at Cassville, Georgia, and died of disease in prison in January 1865. TROIANI COLLECTION.

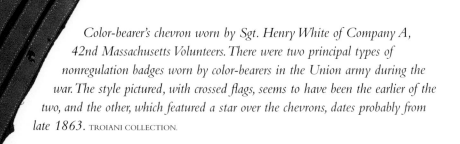

Color-bearer's chevron worn by Sgt. Henry White of Company A, 42nd Massachusetts Volunteers. There were two principal types of nonregulation badges worn by color-bearers in the Union army during the war. The style pictured, with crossed flags, seems to have been the earlier of the two, and the other, which featured a star over the chevrons, dates probably from late 1863. TROIANI COLLECTION.

PRIVATE, 20TH TENNESSEE INFANTRY, C.S.A., SUMMER 1863

The 20th Tennessee Infantry was raised in the northern part of the state in the summer of 1861. The regiment saw its first real action at the battle of Shiloh in April 1862 and fought as part of the Confederate Army of Tennessee for the remainder of the war. In May 1863, the regiment was on the receiving end of the first real use of repeating rifles in battle. At Hoover's Gap, southeast of Murfreesboro, Tennessee, the 20th was part of the force attacking the Union Lightning Brigade, which had recently been armed with Spencer rifles.

Regimental records show a steady supply of uniform items to the 20th, including jackets and, unlike many Confederate regiments, always hats. Also unlike most Southern units, this regiment wore a small brass badge on the hat or coat bearing the regimental designation. As a general rule, the Army of Tennessee received clothing and ordnance from depots in the Deep South such as Columbus and Macon, Georgia. The soldier shown here wears a jacket of the type manufactured at the Columbus facility and is armed with an Enfield rifle. The regiment had been initially armed with flintlock muskets, which were replaced by more modern weapons during 1862. The recorded personal effects of a private of Company E who died on March 4, 1863, were probably typical of those of this regiment:

1 knapsack	1 pair pants
2 coverlets	1 pair boots
2 hats	1 pair socks
3 pair drawers	1 silver watch
2 shirts	1 pocket book, containing $71.00 paper money

PAUL SCHIERL

UNION INFANTRY DRUMMER, WINTER 1863–64

Despite the cold, winter for the Civil War soldier meant at least some rest from marching and the constant threat of battle. Entire armies moved into winter quarters, and picket duty, drill, and parades became the order of the day. Because of the necessity for quick audible communications, the skills of the drummer were required on a daily basis. One particular duty was the beating of reveille each morning. On a cold winter morning, the warmth given by the single-breasted, heavy woolen overcoat with its stand-up collar was more than welcome. The coat for infantry use had an elbow-length cape that added an extra layer of protection to the shoulders and could be pulled over the head to protect the wearer from wind and snow. As gloves were not an item of issue, the extralarge cuffs on the coat could be turned down to cover the hands. Regulations called for the overcoats, or greatcoats, to be made of blue-gray material. Those made for general issue during the war were of sky blue kersey, the same material used for trousers. In some cases, material that was judged too dark in color for trousers was directed to be used for overcoats.

The red cloth corps badge on this drummer's forage cap identifies him as a member of a regiment attached to the 1st Division, III Corps, Army of the Potomac. The men of this division had sent their overcoats to Washington for storage prior to the spring campaign and did not receive them back until late November.

Regulation sky blue Federal overcoat worn by Pvt. Edgar S. Yergason of Company A, 22nd Connecticut Volunteers. It was made in 1862 of satinette, a wool-cotton mix, instead of the specified kersey. In an industrious endeavor to waterproof his overcoat, Private Yergason added beneath his cape a lining cut from a rubberized blanket. TROIANI COLLECTION.

Drum of Pvt. John A. Whitney, Company A, 10th Connecticut Volunteers. It was made by Samuel & Otley of New York City. Many state units used their own painted devices in lieu of the regulation eagle. MUSEUM OF CONNECTICUT HISTORY.

Drumsticks with brass holder for wear on either a sling or a hoop of the drum. The holder was a direct copy of the French model shown in drawings of regulation French equipage as early as 1828. TROIANI COLLECTION.

FÉLIX HECQET, TRACÉ DESCRIPTIF DES DIVERS OBJECTS D'HABILLEMENT, D'ÉQUIPEMENT, DE HARNACHEMENT À L'USAGE DE L'ARMÉE FRANÇAISE EN 1828 (NANTES, FRANCE: EDITIONS D. CANONNIER, 1998), 27.

Kearny Cross medal presented to Sgt. Charles P. Post of Company A, 57th Pennsylvania Volunteer Infantry. These awards were presented by Gen. David Bell Birney in a ceremony on May 27, 1863, to soldiers of the 1st Division, III Corps, who had distinguished themselves. BRUCE HERMANN.

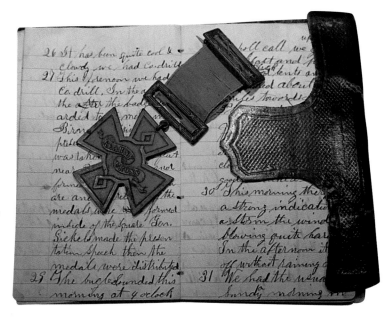

THE GRAY WALL

The miracle accomplished by the Confederate Ordnance and Quartermaster Departments in building an adequate and efficient system of manufacture and supply was a major factor in keeping Southern armies in the field and fighting for four years. Overcoming initial problems, the Confederate government from mid-1862 to late 1864 was able to produce or import in quantity nearly every item needed by its armies. Once the Union naval blockade of Southern ports, combined with the disruption of rail service by advancing Federal armies, began to take its toll, the Confederate soldier began to feel true want. The Army of Tennessee was without a doubt the hardest hit. Following Hood's disastrous advance on Nashville in December 1864, this army found itself lacking in nearly every area of supply. Uniforms, which had been an item of regular issue from depots in Georgia and Alabama, could not now reach the Southern soldiers. Wearing captured Federal items and a mixture of Confederate issue, they continued to make up in courage and determination what they now lacked in matériel. For the Army of Tennessee, as well as the Confederacy, the days were numbered.

This light gray-brown jean cloth Confederate jacket, with locally manufactured Louisiana buttons, was worn by an Englishman who served in the Confederate army. In 1905, he donated his jacket to the Royal Artillery Museum in Woolwich, England, where it remained until the late 1990s, when it returned to this country. TROIANI COLLECTION.

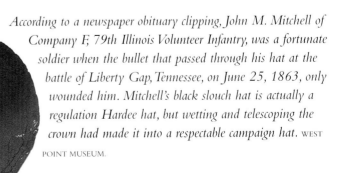

According to a newspaper obituary clipping, John M. Mitchell of Company F, 79th Illinois Volunteer Infantry, was a fortunate soldier when the bullet that passed through his hat at the battle of Liberty Gap, Tennessee, on June 25, 1863, only wounded him. Mitchell's black slouch hat is actually a regulation Hardee hat, but wetting and telescoping the crown had made it into a respectable campaign hat. WEST POINT MUSEUM.

1ST AND 2ND MARYLAND

Although most Confederate soldiers were supposedly ragged and unkempt by 1863, the men of the Maryland Infantry of Robert E. Lee's Army of Northern Virginia were noted for their uniformity. On the road to Gettysburg, a Northern civilian remarked, "They have been telling us you rebs were a ragged set, but you seem to have pretty good clothes; and that you were badly armed . . . but you have good guns, and what's funny to me, all of them have U.S. on them." The Marylander who recorded this quote summed it up by stating, "Our regiment was better clothed than most and all our guns had been captured on battlefields."

From the very start of the war, the Marylanders were characterized by their short gray jackets and caps, or kepis, rather than the common butternut clothes and slouch hats. In 1861, when six companies of Marylanders, raised at Harpers Ferry, marched into Winchester, Virginia, to join companies from Richmond, the shout went up, "Lookout [sic] for you[r] baggage, boys, the Plug-Uglies are coming." The hastily

Confederate forage cap of light-colored or butternut jean cloth material, with a thin leather visor. COLLECTION OF NEW YORK STATE DIVISION OF MILITARY AND NAVAL AFFAIRS.

Confederate sergeant's jacket made of gray-brown jean cloth material. The facings on the cuff are unusual in that they are only on the outside of the sleeve. Instead of the more familiar brass buttons, this coat has wooden buttons, which, though equally functional, were somewhat less martial in character. NELSONIAN INSTITUTE.

equipped men from Harpers Ferry were described as "poorly clad and . . . unkempt and unwashed." Jane Claudia Johnson, wife of Maj. Bradley T. Johnson of the newly formed Maryland battalion, would not have her husband's men present such an appearance, so she raised $10,000 to clothe and equip the men herself. Thereafter the men of the 1st Maryland—and as they became later, the 2nd Maryland—were noted for the quality of their dress, arms, and military bearing.

By 1864, with Confederate resources stretched to nearly the breaking point, the Maryland battalion still drew and wore issue clothing, including Richmond Depot jackets and occasionally clothing from North Carolina, or clothes sent from home and smuggled through Union lines. In August 1864, one Union officer noted Maryland prisoners wearing "little kepis, half grey and half sky-blue," of the regulation style. The men of the Maryland battalion fought notably at Gettysburg and through the battles of 1864, being reduced to an effective strength of 100 men in 1865, 32 of whom were captured when Petersburg was abandoned, leaving only 63 officers and men to surrender at Appomattox.

GEN. PATRICK R. CLEBURNE

November 30, 1864, can be counted as one of the darkest days in the military history of the Confederacy. It was on this day, near the town of Franklin, Tennessee, that the Army of Tennessee lost one of its most dynamic and aggressive leaders, Gen. Patrick R. Cleburne. In a desperate attack, with the regimental battle flags of his division held high behind him, Cleburne fell as he crossed the last line of Union breastworks.

The uniform he wore on this fateful day befitted a man of action. Rather than the conventional dress of high command, he preferred the less formal, looser-fitting officer's sack coat, suitably adorned with the emblems of his rank. He wore his gold-braided general's kepi, securely held by the chinstrap, pushed back on his head. The men of his division, most uniformed in jackets fashioned by the depots in Georgia and Alabama, followed their gallant commander, showing the same brave determination. Only darkness ended the desperate struggle, which saw some of the most savage hand-to-hand fighting of the war.

One of approximately 331 all-iron saber bayonets made at the Tyler (Texas) Ordnance Works between November 1863 and May 1864. With English-manufactured belt frog. A. H. SIEBEL, JR., COLLECTION.

JOHN M. MURPHY AND HOWARD MICHAEL MADAUS, *CONFEDERATE RIFLES AND MUSKETS* (NEWPORT BEACH, CALIF.: GRAPHIC, 1996), 706–7.

PRIVATE, 29TH ALABAMA INFANTRY, SPRING 1864

In the spring of 1864, the 29th Alabama Infantry was one of the best of the veteran regiments of the Confederate Army of the Mississippi. Ahead of it lay transfer to the Army of Tennessee and the fateful campaigns of the summer. By the end of the year, names of battles such as Peach Tree Creek and Franklin would forever be burned into the memory of those lucky enough to survive.

The uniform of the regiment was typical of those issued to Confederate troops serving in the Western armies. The soldier shown here wears a jacket and trousers received from the Columbus, Georgia, Depot, one of the main supply sources for troops in this theater of the war. The 29th had received several issues of clothing in late 1863 and early 1864, including jackets, caps, and a few hats. The regiment was armed with the Enfield rifle musket and carried both English and Confederate-made accoutrements. By midwar, the Confederate supply system, including items of domestic manufacture and imports from both England and Austria, was able to sustain the soldiers to a remarkable degree. The cedar canteen carried by this soldier is likely a product of the Montgomery Arsenal, which produced large numbers of this essential item for the Western armies. While in the West, shoes remained a problem; almost everything else, though at times not abundant, was supplied in quantities adequate to meet the need.

A statement of ordnance and ordnance stores lost and expended in battle by the 29th Alabama from May 9 to June 30, 1864, attests to the hard fighting that lay ahead:

220 Enfield rifles	256 cap pouches
586 bayonets	562 knapsacks
261 cartridge boxes	276 haversacks
270 shoulder belts	388 canteens
250 waist belts	81,453 cartridges
	cal. .577
307 bayonet	74,452 musket
scabbards	caps

DAVID RANKIN, JR.

LONGSTREET'S CORPS, SEPTEMBER 1863

"They Are Certainly Superior to the
Troops of the Army of Tennessee
in Dress"

The retreat of Robert E. Lee's army from Gettysburg and the surrender of the Rebel stronghold at Vicksburg, Mississippi, both in early July 1863, left the Confederates looking for an opportunity to strike back at the Federal army. Confederate president Jefferson Davis decided that the place would be southern Tennessee. The plan was to reinforce Gen. Braxton Bragg's Army of Tennessee and force a rout of the Union Army of the Cumberland under Maj. Gen. William S. Rosecrans. Rosecrans's brilliant Tallahoma campaign from June to August 1863 had succeeded in flanking Bragg out of middle Tennessee. Federal forces were now in possession of Chattanooga, the door to the Deep South.

Included in these Confederate reinforcements were two divisions of Gen. James Longstreet's Corps of the Army of Northern Virginia, those of John Bell Hood and Lafayette McLaws. Before leaving Virginia, Longstreet promised his commander, Robert E. Lee, that he would defeat Rosecrans or die. Longstreet and his veterans were going west looking for a battle, and they found one at Chickamauga Creek.

Descriptions of Longstreet's Corps upon their arrival and during the battle of Chickamauga, September 19–20, 1863, found them to be uniformed differently and in sharp contrast to the Western army soldiers under General Bragg. One of Bragg's artillerymen took special notice of the Easterners' uniformity in appearance: "Our first impression was partly caused by the color of their uniform [dark blue-gray jackets, light blue pants] . . . the superior style of their equipments, in haversacks, canteens, and knapsacks. The contrast between them and General Bragg's motley, ragged

An oval, embossed brass Confederate enlisted man's waist belt buckle of a type favored mostly in the Western Theater. NELSONIAN INSTITUTE.

Butternut-colored jean cloth frock coat with Confederate block "I" buttons, worn 1861–62 by Charles Herbest, Company I, 2nd Kentucky Volunteers, of the famed Orphan Brigade. Herbest was captured at Fort Donelson. After being exchanged, he fought with the Army of Tennessee until its surrender in 1865. M. CUNNINGHAM COLLECTION.

troops was striking in the extreme!" Bragg's soldiers, lamented one Western officer, "never looked worse. Three weeks of maneuvering in the densest dust [during the Tullahoma campaign] without washing, had conferred the same color upon everything!" Bragg's Westerners were described as generally "greasy, dirty, raggedy, barefooted, and wearing go-as-you please . . . with every imaginable variety of garments and head coverings," wearing practically "no uniform at all." Bragg's soldiers preferred to wear clothing sent from home rather than that issued by the Confederate Quartermaster Department.

A member of Kershaw's Brigade of Longstreet's Corps remembered his uniform as a "dark blue round jacket, closely fitting, with light blue trousers: [it] closely resembled those worn by the enemy." The jacket, from several accounts, was a dark bluish gray. It is believed that the jackets, trousers, and caps were produced in Richmond and issued through the Confederate Quartermaster Department. The dark blue and light blue cloth had possibly come through on blockade runners from England, some of it arriving as early as February 1863.

A soldier in the 2nd Georgia Infantry, Benning's Brigade, Longstreet's Corps, wrote, "Sometimes the government would get a supply . . . of fine English cloth, and we would get good uniforms, almost to blue." This same soldier was fired upon by his own friends in Tennessee, "So blue [like Yankees] did we appear." Even the Federals had trouble distinguishing Longstreet's men from their own. Lt. Charles Clark of the 125th Ohio Volunteer Infantry, awaiting the attack of Kershaw's Brigade, heard the order, "Cease fire! . . . they are McCooks [Union] troops!" He noted that Kershaw's Confederates "appeared at a distance to wear blue, dusty blue. We had never seen a Confederate soldier clothed otherwise

This superbly made British Army style shoe never made it to the Confederacy, where it was so desperately needed. Captured from a blockade runner, it was preserved as a trophy of war. Note the iron heel plate and hobnailed sole. "English regulation shoes" were advertised at auction in Augusta, Georgia, in the May 14, 1863, Augusta Chronicle and Sentinel, *selling at $6 per pair.* COLLECTION OF NEW YORK STATE DIVISION OF MILITARY AND NAVAL AFFAIRS.

These rugged Confederate soldier's shoes were recovered after fighting near the Southside Railroad, Petersburg, Virginia. Although patterned on the Federal brogan, they are strictly of Southern manufacture, being made of undyed leather with crude pegging on the soles. Although not attractive, they were sturdy enough to get the soldier where he needed to go. COLLECTION OF NEW YORK STATE DIVISION OF MILITARY AND NAVAL AFFAIRS.

than in butternut or gray." A volley by the Confederates ended the debate, but many a Federal soldier, and Rebel as well, seemed confused by the appearance of Longstreet's men.

Gen. Ulysses S. Grant made the same mistake. Grant had been ordered to Chattanooga to help reverse the fortunes of the Federal army, which now found itself under siege after Chickamauga. He described a confusing encounter on an inspection tour of the picket lines surrounding Chattanooga:

> [T]he most friendly relations seemed to exist between the pickets of the two armies. At one place a tree which had fallen across the stream was used by the soldiers of both armies in drawing water for their camps. General Longstreet's Corps was stationed there at the time, and wore the blue of a little different shade from our uniform. Seeing a

soldier in blue on the log, I rode up to him, commenced conversing with him, and asked whose Corps he belonged to. He was very polite, touching his hat to me, said he belonged to Longstreet's Corps. I asked him a few questions, but not with a view of gaining any particular information—all of which he answered, and I rode off.

Longstreet left the Army of Tennessee in early November and marched east toward Knoxville. In what became known as the Knoxville campaign, Longstreet's men were in bare feet and rags when they returned to Lee's army in the early spring of 1864. The quartermaster general of the Confederacy wanted no more light blue pants, stating that "gray makes up better." Perhaps it was better not to be shot at by one's own men.

76TH OHIO VOLUNTEER INFANTRY

It is often assumed that all Confederate soldiers were ragged and in need of uniforms and that, conversely, all Union soldiers were well clothed with luxurious uniforms. The truth is that the rigors of campaigning wreaked havoc on North and South alike. One soldier of the 76th Ohio wrote, during the Vicksburg campaign, that he was indeed ragged: "The shirt I had on was gone all but the front and one sleeve . . . my blouse all rags, and my only respectable covering a forage cap." By the time his knapsack with spare clothing caught up to him, he reported, "My pants had lost all covering qualities and I had thrown them away, compelled for a day or two to serve my country garbed in underwear only."

The 76th Ohio Volunteer Infantry was organized and mustered in at Camp Sherman, Newark, Ohio, from October 1861 to February 1862. The regiment was uniformed in standard Federal uniforms for much of its service. The uniform was remembered as "a dark blue blouse, light blue pants, forage caps, low, broad soled shoes ('bootees' the government styled them) and blue overcoat with cape. Each soldier carried a gray woolen blanket and a rubber blanket." After two years of hard campaigning in the West, the 76th became a veteran regiment in January 1864. To celebrate this status, the veterans of the 76th bought themselves a new and colorful uniform:

RON TUNISON

On the 27th [of January] the officers held a meeting to discuss the adoption of a new uniform for the Regiment. It was deemed desirable that the veterans be all clothed alike with some kind of a zouave jacket that they might make a fine appearance on their return to Ohio. A Regimental fund of about seven hundred dollars had been created which it was considered best to expend for this purpose. The officers decided on the style most appropriate to be a short dark blue jacket with rounded corners, no collar and trimmed in sky-blue binding.

The new uniform was contracted for in Cincinnati and was ready when the regiment arrived at that city prior to its veteran furlough.

The 76th was originally armed with "old second-hand Belgian rifles, a short, heavy, clumsy arm with a vicious recoil." In December 1862, however, the men received Springfield rifle muskets, which they retained through the rest of their service. Armed with Springfields and standard accoutrements, even noncommissioned officers' swords with shoulder belts in Company G, only the veterans' furlough jackets distinguished the 76th from other regiments of the XV Corps.

Federal forage cap of the 10th Vermont, with insignia of the 3rd Division, VI Army Corps. TROIANI COLLECTION.

Although referred to as a Burnside hat in a period military goods catalog, there seems to be no evidence that famed Gen. Ambrose E. Burnside ever wore one. This low-crowned officer's slouch hat is done up with insignia for an unknown officer of a 4th Regiment of Infantry. TROIANI COLLECTION.

Infantry uniform jacket of Sgt. George H. Snell of the 121st New York Volunteers. The Federal government furnished several hundred thousand of these during the latter part of the war. They were also worn by the men of the Signal Corps. TROIANI COLLECTION.

12TH INDIANA VOLUNTEER INFANTRY, 1864

In December 1863, the 12th Indiana Infantry, in dire need of uniforms after a hard campaign, received an issue of new uniforms made in Indianapolis by a merchant tailor named Joseph Staub. The uniform had a collarless, dark blue wool jacket with a nine-button front, made with a false panel to give the appearance of a Zouave jacket worn over a buttoned vest. The panel was of sky blue kersey edged with white cotton tape. Miniature trefoils of light blue cord on each breast added to the illusion of a Zouave uniform. The regiment's colonel, Reuben Williams, wrote, "We have received our new uniforms manufactured by Staub . . . and present as gay an appearance as any regiment that ever left the State."

Not everyone in the regiment was as appreciative of the new jackets, however. Sgt. John Shultz wrote home: "Our jackets have arrived. The boys pronounce them a *Grand Bore* for they are not worth half the price 6.25 and are more style and show than worth." Indeed, they must have been very unpopular, for Lt. Col. James Goodenow published the following order: "Commanders of companies will see that the *New Uniform*[s] recently issued to the men of this Regiment are not to be disposed of under any circumstances whatever. The different companies will be made acquainted with the purport of this order at the first subsequent roll call after which any violations will be reported to this Headquarters."

But the men wore the uniforms, however unpopular they may have been. A surviving jacket was worn at the battle of Resaca, Georgia, where its owner, Sgt. John Shultz, was wounded. Photographs show that the officers also wore the jacket with shoulder straps.

DICK AND M. E. CLOW

HOOD'S TENNESSEE CAMPAIGN, SEPTEMBER TO DECEMBER 1864

The date was September 29, 1864. Confederate general John Bell Hood and 42,000 Confederate soldiers of the Army of Tennessee set off to begin what has become known as Hood's Tennessee campaign, the last great campaign in the Western Theater of the Civil War. It was Hood's plan to draw the Federal forces commanded by William Tecumseh Sherman away from Atlanta by threatening Sherman's lines of supply. General Sherman did follow Hood for a time, but

Confederate cast pewter buckle with iron wire hooks soldered to the back, found on the battlefield of Knoxville, Tennessee, by a Michigan soldier. TROIANI COLLECTION.

then he turned South to begin his famous March to the Sea. That left Maj. Gen. George H. Thomas and his Union troops in Nashville to deal with Hood.

Descriptions of Hood's Army of Tennessee for late 1864 are many. Because Hood continually changed directions as he moved North, few supplies reached his army. By necessity, the Confederates were forced to use the food and captured clothing of their enemies. They had bare feet and ragged uniforms for much of the campaign. A Union private of the 14th Illinois Infantry captured near Moon's Station, Georgia, made note that the Confederates "made all kinds of one-sided trades for our clothing, hats, boots, and shoes." From Big Shanty, this same Union prisoner watched as Hood's entire army marched past him on their way to Dalton, Georgia. He described the Confederates as "poorly clad in brown and gray cotton suits, and but for the flags they carried, might have been a section of the old Continental Army."

A Union captain captured at Dalton also remarked as Hood's entire army marched by. "They were ragged and thinly clad, having as a general thing, only pantaloons, shirt, and hat in their inventory of clothing. Their pantaloons were greasy and tattered, the shirts, shocking affairs in multitudinous variety. As a general thing they were liberally shod, though in Stewart's Division . . . over three hundred were without shoes. Not more than one in ten had blankets."

By the time Hood's Confederates reached Tuscumbia, Alabama, on October 31, an artilleryman in Guibor's Battery found his comrades to be "rather ragged, and many . . . bare-footed." To cover their feet, some soldiers began to make moccasins out of rawhide from slaughtered cattle. To add to

their discomfort, a cold, chilly rain began to fall, turning the roads to slippery mud. "The boys who wore moccasins had a good deal of trouble keeping them on when they got wet," remembered one Alabama infantryman.

Hood and his men made contact with a sizable Union force near Columbia, Tennessee. The Confederates' pursuit resulted in the bloody battle of Franklin, Tennessee, on November 30, 1864. Many of the Confederate prisoners captured at Franklin were in Union clothing, as described by Pvt. Adam J. Weaver of the 104th Ohio. "The Rebel prisoners are nearly all wearing parts of our uniforms . . . especially our shoes [and] overcoats. . . . They still retain their droopy felt hats which gives them a hayseedy look."

Hood followed the Federals to Nashville and laid siege to the city. On December 15 and 16, the Federals attacked, breaking Hood's lines and turning the ensuing battle into a rout for many Confederates. Hood's army moved south from Nashville, ending their retreat at Tupelo, Mississippi, on January 3, 1865. Only 17,709 soldiers and officers were reported as present for duty. A Confederate officer in Walthall's Division wrote home that "the Army cannot muster 5,000 effectives [out of 17,000]. Nine-tenths of the line officers and men are barefooted and naked . . . and many go home every day never to return."

On January 13, Hood resigned. What was left of the Army of Tennessee was shipped east to fight Sherman in North Carolina. In March 1865, an official count listed only 6,745 men as present for duty. Of that number, 2,298 had no shoes. What an end for the once magnificent Army of Tennessee!

*Butternut-colored jean cloth Confederate uniform jacket
worn by John C. Zehring of Company A (Shelby Grays),
4th Tennessee Regiment. Possibly a product of the Milledgeville,
Georgia, Depot, Zehring's clothing issuances indicate that he probably
received this jacket in the spring of 1865.* THE HORSE SOLDIER.

*Pair of unfinished soldier's wooden-soled canvas shoes taken from
Confederate quartermaster stores in Atlanta, where they were found in
great quantities. Because of critical leather shortages, the
Southern manufacturers were reduced to such drastic
measures to keep their armies shod.* COLLECTION
OF NEW YORK STATE DIVISION OF MILITARY AND NAVAL
AFFAIRS.

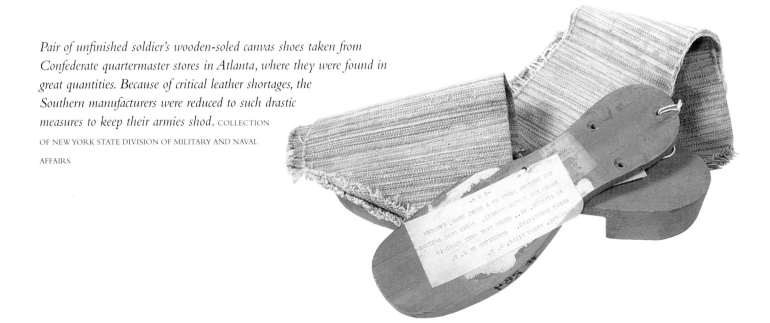

203RD PENNSYLVANIA INFANTRY, PRIVATE, FALL 1864

By 1864, the inducement of special uniforms to aid in the formation of new regiments had all but disappeared. An exception was the 203rd Pennsylvania Infantry. With the backing of Maj. Gen. David B. Birney, this regiment would be known as Birney's Sharpshooters and would wear the uniform of the famous Berdan's Sharpshooters. The new regiment began enlistment in September 1864, at a time when the original Sharpshooters had all but passed out of existence. Since 1862, the Union army Quartermaster Department had supplied the distinctive green uniform that, along with their legendary shooting skills, had been the hallmark of Berdan's regiments. Now, in the fall of 1864, there were more green uniforms on hand than there were men to wear them.

The 203rd received the remaining stock of green frock coats and trousers, along with a few caps. This issue was supplemented by newly made items, just as had been the practice for the past three years. Unlike the Sharpshooters of 1861, who had received the Sharps breech-loading rifle, the men of the 203rd were issued the Springfield rifle musket, most likely the improved model of 1864. Their accoutrements included the 1864 model cartridge box with an embossed "US" within an oval pattern, reminiscent of the brass plate previously issued. This box was suspended from a black leather cross belt, but unlike that issued to Berdan's men, it was no longer adorned with the familiar round brass plate with the raised eagle. Both brass

WILLIAM RODEN

plates had been discontinued by the Ordnance Department as serving no purpose. These plates had been disliked by Berdan's men, who would have been more than happy to see them go.

Other than these variations, the enlisted men of the 203rd, from their leather leggings to their green caps, appeared as nearly exact copies of the original Sharpshooters. Only the badges of the X Army Corps, along with the brass letters and numbers adorning their caps, served to set them apart. The officers of the 203rd, as those in Berdan's regiments, wore regulation blue with the badges of rank, such as

trouser stripes, of green. The famous uniforms brought with them an image that belied their inexperience. It was up to the officers and men of the new regiment to prove themselves.

Their chance came in January of the new year. Serving not as sharpshooters, but as line infantry, the 203rd made up part of the force designated to assault the Confederate stronghold at the mouth of North Carolina's Cape Fear River, known as Fort Fisher. On January 15, 1865, during this attack, the regiment suffered heavy losses, including both its colonel and lieutenant colonel, who were killed inside the Confederate works.

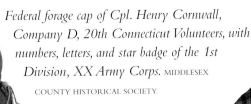

Federal forage cap of Cpl. Henry Cornwall, Company D, 20th Connecticut Volunteers, with numbers, letters, and star badge of the 1st Division, XX Army Corps. MIDDLESEX COUNTY HISTORICAL SOCIETY.

One of several plaid flannel shirts made by the mother of Pvt. Edgar S. Yergason of Company A, 22nd Connecticut Volunteers, and sent to him during his term of active service. Because of the roughness of government undergarments, soldiers often preferred to provide their own whenever possible. As one soldier explained: "[T]he shirt [Army issue] was—well, a revelation to most of us both as to size and shape and material. It was so rough, that no living mortal, probably could wear it, except perhaps one who wished to do penance by wearing a hair shirt. Mine was promptly sent home . . . with the request that it be kept as a sort of heirloom in the family for future generations to wonder at." TROIANI COLLECTION.

HARRY M. KIEFFER, *THE RECOLLECTIONS OF A DRUMMER-BOY* (BOSTON: JAMES R. OSGOOD, 1883), 40–41.

Presumably, Sgt. Stephen H. Parker of Company D, 59th Massachusetts Volunteers, had left this custom-made dress coat behind in camp or storage when he was killed in the disastrous assault on the Crater at Petersburg on July 30, 1864. The coat bears service stripes on the lower sleeves, as Parker was a veteran of prior service in another regiment. TROIANI COLLECTION.

Appomattox Courthouse, April 12, 1865

The formal surrender of Robert E. Lee's Confederate Army of Northern Virginia took place on April 12, 1865, at Appomattox Courthouse, Virginia. As the marching columns of gray-clad soldiers ceremoniously turned to face the Federals, the Confederates were ordered to fix bayonets, stack arms, undo and hang up their accoutrements, and lean their battle flags on the stacked guns. All was quiet during the ceremony. One Confederate soldier remembered, "We said nothing . . . neither did they say anything to us."

The prevailing mood of the Confederate officers supervising the surrender was one of sad disappointment and humiliation. Finally, when the last Confederate unit passed in line, a Union soldier cried out from the ranks, "Three cheers for the last Brigade!" "This soldierly generosity was more than we could bear," recalled a Southern officer, "Many of the grizzled veterans wept like children, and my own eyes were as blind, as my voice was dumb."

Descriptions of the appearance of the Confederates in the closing days of the Civil War are many. A Union soldier remarked that the Rebel soldiers he saw "were mostly in homespun butternut colored jean cloth, with no semblance of uniform. [It was] hard to distinguish betwixt the officers and the privates as they are all dressed alike." Another Federal remembered the soldiers of the Army of Northern Virginia as a collection of "dirty, battered, ranks of soldiers, none of them well clad, and nearly all the officers in fatigue dress."

The change in dress for the Confederate officers from a fine gray frock trimmed with gold lace to the uniform of a private went back two years, to the fall of 1863. Higher costs for uniforms and the materials needed to produce them had risen to the point of being unaffordable to many. The schedule of prices that accompanied a resolution for assistance by the staff of Bates Brigade, Army of Tennessee, to the Confederate Congress, showed that in late 1863, the average charge for a tailored officer's frock was $350; boots, $250; pants, $125; hat, $80 to $125; shirt, $50; underdrawers, $15; and socks, $10. This meant that a new officer's uniform cost over

DAVID RANKIN, JR.

$980, when the monthly pay for a new second lieutenant was just $80 a month!

On March 6, 1864, as a remedy, General Orders No. 28 was issued out of Richmond. It stated that all commissioned officers would now be allowed to purchase privates' clothing, and cloth for clothing, from any quartermaster at the price it cost the government. Confederate officers were also entitled to one food ration in kind, the same as privates, for their mess.

A special congressional committee looking into the issue of officers' clothing found that for the latter half of 1864, 31,940 yards of fine-grade cloth for uniforms was purchased through the Quartermaster Department. Only a small portion of it, however, actually went to the line officers. The

This type of rectangular "C.S.A." belt plate was believed to have been a product of the Atlanta Arsenal. Although widely issued to the Army of Tennessee, some were issued to Longstreet's Corps, which was serving in the Western Theater in 1863–64. WILLIAM ERQUITT COLLECTION.

Pvt. John A. Dolan of Austin's Battalion of Louisiana Sharphooters wore this jacket in 1865. A simple five-button jean cloth jacket with exterior pocket and blue collar, it is one of those believed made for Richard Taylor's Department of Alabama, Mississippi, and East Louisiana. CONFEDERATE MEMORIAL HALL, CLAUDE LEVET PHOTOGRAPH.

Confederate officer's waist belt constructed of unpainted canvas with remains of russet leather sword straps. As leather became scarce in the South, substitute materials became more prevalent. TROIANI COLLECTION.

largest portion went to those serving in the rear echelon areas. No provisions were made by the Quartermaster Department to get the higher-grade cloth to those officers serving near the front lines.

Quartermaster General Alexander Robert Lawton informed the special committee that affordable officers' uniforms, 1,000 in number, were now being made up in Montgomery, Alabama, for Lee's command. Provision for 6,000 other officers was accomplished for the second half of 1864. Officers' uniforms were now to be supplied from the Quartermaster Department.

Many did not or could not procure the regulation dress frock, trousers, boots, and cap appropriate for their rank. By necessity, the uniform of a private, consisting of short jeans jacket and trousers, hat or cap, and a good pair of shoes, made a cheap and durable outfit. The only sign of rank was a sword, pistol, and maybe some lace on the collar denoting the grade of lieutenant or captain.

A Confederate staffer described their dress toward the end of the war: "My equipment was a blanket rolled up and carried across my shoulder, and it contained a change of underclothes. . . . Towards the last days we were almost barefoot. . . . As to hats, their variety and material was marvelous. . . . When it came to jackets and trousers, the least said is the easiest understood. They were conspicuous by their fluttering raggedness."

PRIVATE, 2ND MARYLAND INFANTRY C.S.A., 1864

By 1864, the style of dress within the ranks of the Army of Northern Virginia had, by necessity if not by design, reached a high degree of standardization. The waist length jacket was worn by nearly all of those who marched in Lee's army. The kepi was widely used and even the arms and accoutrements, though still mixed in type and design, had taken on a sameness that was a far contrast from the early days of the war. Contributing to this was the successful importation of clothing from England and Ireland. This Marylander has been uniformed in one of the thousands of jackets received on the contract with Peter Tait of Limerick, Ireland. He has maintained a degree of individuality by replacing the issued buttons with those of his home state. His kepi shows the blue infantry trim. Overall he stands in sharp contrast to the traditional image of Confederate soldiers dressed in rags during the final months of the war.

The 2nd Maryland was part of the proud Second Corps of the Army of Northern Virginia. In February 1865, the Second Corps Quartermaster, Maj. George D. Mercer made the following report to Col. James L. Corley, Chief Quartermaster of the Army:

DICK AND M. E. CLOW

Office Chief Q.M. 2nd Corps
February 2, 1865

Colonel:
    From an examination of the Inspection Report, I find that the troops of this Corps are represented as still requiring a large amount of clothing. This is an error, which I have corrected upon the report, by an endorsement. With the exception of a few pants and shirts the estimates forwarded on the 1st of January 65 have been very nearly filled.
    From the quantity of clothing issued during the past two months the troops ought to be well clothed.

                        D. Mercer
                        Maj. and Acting Corps Q.M.

Pair of Union soldier's mittens of blue and white mixed yarn, with extra trigger finger. These were produced by women at home for contractors, using printed government patterns and specifications. TROIANI COLLECTION.

Exquisite silver VI Army Corps badges taken from the body of Lt. Col. John Wilson of the 43rd New York Volunteers on the Spotsylvania battlefield by a Confederate soldier. They were returned to his family after the war. COLLECTION OF NEW YORK STATE DIVISION OF MILITARY AND NAVAL AFFAIRS.

Lt. Col. Edward L. Gaul
wore this black braided kepi during his service with the 159th New York Volunteers until his discharge at Morganza, Louisiana, due to illness. It bears the regulation gold-embroidered infantry horn with silver numeral 159. TROIANI COLLECTION.

Federal officers serving with mounted troops were allowed by regulation a short, dark blue jacket. Many officers of all branches chose this option, and the range of variations is boundless. This example, worn by Col. Ezra Carmen of the 13th New Jersey Volunteers, is buttoned with a congested row of twenty-one small eagle buttons. TROIANI COLLECTION.

SOURCES

THE INFANTRY

INTRODUCTION

1. National Archives, Record Group 393, entry 202, III Army Corps, Letters, Orders, and Reports, 1862–64.
2. Ibid., Record Group 94, Regimental Books, 53rd Pennsylvania Infantry.
3. Ibid., Record Group 109, M-374 and M-269, Service Records of the 19th Alabama and 17th Mississippi Infantry Regiments.
4. Ibid., M-331, Compiled Service Records of Confederate General and Staff Officers, Maj. John F. Lay, Assistant Inspector General.
5. Ibid., Record Group 94, Regimental Papers, 5th Michigan Infantry.
6. Ibid., Record Group 109, M-437, Letters Received by the Confederate Secretary of War.
7. Ibid., Record Group 92, entry 2182, January 2, 1862, Letter from Quartermaster General in re General Orders 101.
8. Editors of Time-Life Books, *Echoes of Glory: Arms and Equipment of the Confederate Army* (Alexandria, Va.: Time-Life Books, 1991).
9. National Archives, Record Group 109, M-324, Compiled Service Records of Confederate Soldiers from Virginia, Papers of 53rd Virginia Infantry.
10. Ibid., Record Group 92, entry 999, Letters Sent Relating to Clothing and Equipage, Volume 22, Letter Sent by Wm. G. LeDuc, Lieutenant Colonel and Chief Quartermaster, 11th Corps.
11. Ibid. Record Group 109, M-324, Papers of the 53rd Virginia Infantry.
12. Ibid. Record Group 92, entry 999, Letters Sent Relating to Clothing and Equipage, Volume 22, Le Duc Letter.
13. Ibid., Record Group 109, M-226, Compiled Service Records of Confederate Soldiers from Georgia, 4th Georgia Infantry.
14. Editors of Time-Life Books, *Echoes of Glory*.
15. National Archives, Record Group 109, M-437, Tait Letter.
16. Ibid., Record Group 92, Quartermaster Consolidated Correspondence File, B. G. Badger to Joseph Baggot, Headquarters, Army of the Potomac, March 21, 1863.
17. Ibid., Record Group 94, Regimental Order Book, 147th Pennsylvania Infantry, Order from 1st Brigade, 2nd Division, XII Corps.

CORPORAL, 16TH NEW YORK INFANTRY, JUNE 1862

Eugene Miller and Forrest F. Steinlage, *Der Turner Soldat: Diary of Erland Futter* (Louisville, Ky.: Calmar Publications, 1988), 91.
Newton Martin Curtis, *From Bull Run to Chancellorsville* (New York: G. P. Putnam's Sons, 1906) 114–15.

19TH TENNESSEE INFANTRY, C.S.A., APRIL 1862

Civil War Centennial Commission of Tennessee, *Tennesseans in the Civil War* (Nashville: Civil War Centennial Commission, 1964).
David Sullins, *Recollections of an Old Man* (Bristol, Tenn.: King Printing Co., 1910), 212, 214.
National Archives, Record Group 109, M-268, Military Service Records Various Officers, 19th Tennessee Infantry.

FIRE ON CAROLINE STREET

George A. Bruce, *The Twentieth Regiment of Massachusetts Volunteer Infantry, 1861–1865* (Boston: Houghton, Mifflin, 1906), 49.
Charles F. Walcott, *History of the Twenty-First Regiment Massachusetts Volunteers in the War for the Preservation of the Union, 1861–1865* (Boston: Houghton, Mifflin, 1882), 240.
Photograph of Cpl. Robert Weston, Company A., 20th Massachusetts Volunteers, formerly in the Michael J. McAfee Collection.

12TH TENNESSEE REGIMENT

New York Herald, October 30, 1831.
Nashville Union and American, August 31, 1861.

BURNSIDE'S BRIDGE

Stephen W. Sears, *Landscape Turned Red* (New York: Ticknor & Fields, 1983).
National Archives, Record Group 94, Regimental Papers, 51st Pennsylvania Infantry.
Ibid., Record Group 156, Quarterly Returns of Ordnance and Ordnance Stores on Hand in Regular and Volunteer Army Organizations.
Thomas H. Parker, *Regimental History of the 51st Pennsylvania Infantry* (Philadelphia: King and Baird, 1869).
Frederick H. Dyer, *A Compendium of the War of the Rebellion* (New York: Thomas Yoseloff, 1959).

PRIVATE, 5TH NEW JERSEY INFANTRY, MAY 1863

National Archives, Record Group 94, Regimental Books of the 5th New Jersey Infantry.

Ibid., Record Group 156, Quarterly Returns of Ordnance.

Earl J. Coates and Dean S. Thomas, *An Introduction to Civil War Small Arms* (Gettysburg, Pa.: Thomas Publications, 1990), 91.

The War of the Rebellion: The Official Records of the Union and Confederate Armies, vol. 27, part 1, 575.

Frederick H. Dyer, *A Compendium of the War of the Rebellion* (New York: Thomas Yoseloff, 1959), 1358.

14TH MISSISSIPPI INFANTRY, FORT DONELSON, TENNESSEE, FEBRUARY 18, 1863

Reminiscences of Milton Asbury Ryan, Company B, 14th Mississippi Infantry, Carter House Collection, Franklin, Tennessee.

Memphis (Tennessee) Appeal, February 22, 1862.

Bloomington (Illinois) Pantagraph, February 25, 1862.

Caryle (Illinois) Weekly Reveille, February 23, 1862.

Watertown (Wisconsin) Democrat, March 6, 1862.

13TH PENNSYLVANIA RESERVES

O. E. Howard Thomson and William H. Rauch, *History of the "Bucktails"* (Philadelphia: Electric, 1906).

Edwin A. Glover, *Bucktailed Wildcats* (New York: Thomas Yoseloff, 1960).

THE IRON BRIGADE

O. B. Curtis, *Story of the Twenty-fourth Michigan of the Iron Brigade: Known as the Detroit and Wayne County Regiment* (Detroit: Winn & Hammond, 1891).

21ST OHIO VOLUNTEER INFANTRY, CORPORAL, COMPANY C, SEPTEMBER 1863

National Archives, Record Group 393, part 2, entry 5784, Inspection Reports of the 3rd Brigade, 2nd Division, XIV Corps.

Capt. Silas S. Canfield, *History of the 21st Regiment Ohio Volunteer Infantry* (Toledo: Vrooman, Anderson and Bateman, 1893), 95.

National Archives, Record Group 94, Regimental Books, 21st Ohio Infantry.

TOWARD THE ANGLE

Kathy Georg Harrison and John W. Busey, *Nothing but Glory* (Gettysburg, Pa.: Thomas Publications, 1987), 49.

National Archives, Record Group 92, entry 999, LeDuc Letter, Lieutenant Colonel and Chief, XI Corps Quartermaster.

THE TEXAS BRIGADE, 1863

National Archives, Record Group 109, M-323, Service Records of Soldiers from State of Texas, 1st, 4th, and 5th Texas.

1ST SOUTH CAROLINA VOLUNTEER INFANTRY, U.S. COLORED TROOPS

Frederick H. Dyer, *A Compendium of the War of the Rebellion* (New York: Thomas Yoseloff, 1959), 1636.

Frederick P. Todd, *American Military Equipage, 1851–1872,* vol. 2 (n.p.: Chatham Square, 1983).

National Archives, Record Group 156, M-1281, Summary Statements of Quarterly Returns of Ordnance and Ordnance Stores on Hand in Regular and Volunteer Army Organizations.

27TH VIRGINIA INFANTRY, COLOR SERGEANT, DECEMBER 1862

National Archives, Record Group 109, M-324, Compiled Service Records of Confederate Soldiers Who Served in Organizations from the State of Virginia, 27th Virginia Infantry.

COLONEL OF THE CONFEDERACY

National Archives, Record Group 109, M-437, Letters Received by the Confederate States Secretary of War.

PRIVATE, 53RD GEORGIA INFANTRY, JULY 1863

National Archives, Record Group 109, M-266, Compiled Service Records of Confederate Soldiers Who Served from Georgia, 53rd Georgia.

Editors of Time-Life Books, *Echoes of Glory,* Confederate volume (Alexandria, Va.: Time-Life Books, 1991), 185.

1ST MINNESOTA

National Archives, Record Group 393, part 2, entry 70.

Harry W. Pfanz, *Gettysburg: The Second Day* (Chapel Hill: University of North Carolina Press, 1987), 410.

PRIVATE, 20TH TENNESSEE INFANTRY, C.S.A., SUMMER 1863

National Archives, Record Group 109, M-268, Compiled Service Records of Confederate Soldiers, Tennessee.

Ibid. Service file of Pvt. John A. Sanders, Company E, 20th Tennessee Infantry.

UNION INFANTRY DRUMMER, WINTER 1863–64

National Archives, Record Group 393, part 2, entry 205, Weekly Reports of the Assistant Inspector General to the Headquarters, Army of the Potomac.

1ST AND 2ND MARYLAND

Ross Kimmel, "Enlisted Uniforms of the Maryland Confederate Infantry," parts 1 and 2, *Military Collector and Historian* 41, no. 3 (fall 1989): 98–108; no. 4 (winter 1989): 183–88.

GEN. PATRICK R. CLEBURNE

Richmond Examiner, November 1, 1864.

PRIVATE, 29TH ALABAMA INFANTRY, SPRING 1864

National Archives, Record Group 109, M-311, Compiled Service Records of Confederate Soldiers That Served from Alabama, 29th Alabama.

Ibid., M-331, Compiled Service Records of General and Staff Officers, File of John Ansley, MSK.

Ibid., M-311, Alabama Service Records, File of Samuel Abernathy, Captain, Company E, 29th Alabama.

LONGSTREET'S CORPS, SEPTEMBER 1863

Larry J. Daniel, *Soldier in the Army of Tennessee* (Chapel Hill: University of North Carolina Press, 1991), 11.

John B. Lindsley, *Millitary Annals of Tennessee: Confederate* (Nashville: J. M. Lindsley, 1886), 820–23.

Glenn Tucker, *Bloody Battle in the West* (Dayton, Ohio: Bobbs-Merrill, 1976), 172.

Augustus Dickert, *History of Kershaw's Brigade* (n.p.: Elbert E. Aull, 1899), 268.

W. R. Houghton, *War Record of W. R. Houghton While Serving in Confederate States Army* (Montgomery, Ala.: Paragon Press, 1912), 62.

Charles Clark, *Opdycks Tigers, 125th O.V.I.* (Columbus, Ohio: Spahr & Glenn, 1895), 107.

Ulysses S. Grant, *Personal Memoirs of U. S. Grant* (New York: Charles Webster, 1885) 320–21.

76TH OHIO VOLUNTEER INFANTRY

Charles A. Willison, *A Boy's Service with the 76th Ohio* (Huntington, W.V.: Blue Acorn Press, 1995).

Ordnance Report.

12TH INDIANA VOLUNTEER INFANTRY, 1864

James Spears, "The Zouave Jacket," *Indiana History Bulletin* 40, no. 3 (March 1963): 35–37.

HOOD'S TENNESSEE CAMPAIGN, SEPTEMBER TO DECEMBER 1864

Aaron Smith, *On Wheels and How I Came There* (New York: Eaton and Mains, 1892), 194–95, 200–201.

Richmond Examiner, November 2, 1864.

Samuel B. Dunlap Diary, October 28–November 1, 1864, State Historical Society of Missouri.

T. E. Matthems, 33rd Alabama Memoir, Alabama State Archives.

Wiley Sword, notes sent to author.

The War of the Rebellion: A Compilation of the Official Records of the Union and Confederate Armies (Washington, D.C.: Government Printing Office, 1880–1901), ser. 1, vol. 45, part 1, 733–39.

203RD PENNSYLVANIA INFANTRY, PRIVATE, FALL 1864

National Archives, Record Group 94, Regimental Books, 203rd Pennsylvania Infantry.

Ibid., Record Group 92, entry 2182, Washington Depot to Schuylkill Arsenal, September 23, 1864.

The War of the Rebellion: The Official Records of the Union and Confederate Armies, series I, vol. 46, part 1, 414–21.

APPOMATTOX COURTHOUSE, APRIL 12, 1865

Chris Calkins, *The Final Bivouac: The Surrender Parade at Appomattox and the Disbanding of the Armies, April 10–May 20, 1865* (Lynchburg, Va.: H. E. Howard, 1988), 36, 39, 56, 73.

The War of the Rebellion: A Compilation of the Official Records of the Union and Confederate Armies (Washington, D.C.: Government Printing Office, 1880–1901), vol. 22, pt. 1, 651–67.

S. A. Miller, *Report: Special Committee on Pay and Clothing,* February 11, 1865.

James H. M'Neilly, "Going Out and Coming Back," *Confederate Veteran* 29, no. 8 (August 1921): 288.

PRIVATE, 2ND MARYLAND INFANTRY, C.S.A., 1864

Based on an example in the collection of the Maryland Historical Society.

National Archives, Record Group 109, M-331, Compiled Service Records of Confederate General and Staff Officers, file of George D. Mercer.